NABC's Youth Basketball Coaching Handbook

Beyond
the
Backboard

Jerry Krause and Bruce Brown

COACHES
CHOICE™

ISBN: 1-58518-890-5
Library of Congress Control Number: 2006924906
Cover design: Studio J Art & Design
Book layout: Studio J Art & Design

Coaches Choice
P.O. Box 1828
Monterey, CA 93942
www.coacheschoice.com

Dedication

This book is dedicated to all the men and women who volunteer their time, energy, expertise, and emotions to work with young athletes. For many of those young people, you will be their vision of a "coach" for the remainder of their lives.

Acknowledgments

The authors would like to thank Jim Peterson of Coaches Choice Publishing for bringing our vision of a better sport experience for young basketball players to fruition. We are indebted to the National Association of Basketball Coaches for endorsing and spreading this gospel. We are especially indebted to youth basketball coaches for their time and interest in young people—this book is dedicated to you. Finally, a personal note of gratitude goes to Lisa Mispley, graduate assistant coach at Gonzaga University, for her coaching expertise, basketball interest, and numerous hours dedicated to the development and completion of our manuscript. Similar thanks go to the support staff at Coaches Choice, which has smoothed over the dissimilar writing styles of the coauthors.

—Jerry Krause
—Bruce Brown

Contents

Preface

Coaching youth basketball has two essential prerequisites—a love of young people and a desire to help them develop (physically, mentally, and socially). When a parent or other interested sports person possesses the desire to care for, nurture, and work with youngsters interested in playing the sport of basketball, the next question is "What do I need to know to make it a worthwhile experience for them and for me?"

Technical knowledge of basketball is usually the first answer to this question. It is also the first thing most prospective youth basketball coaches seek out. This technical knowledge typically includes the fundamentals of the game and the development of a fun experience—what skills to teach, when to teach them, and how to teach those skills and modify the game for younger players as they grow and develop.

The most critical background material for coaching youth basketball, though, is centered on coaching youngsters. It has been said that you don't coach basketball, you coach young people who play basketball.

NABC's Youth Basketball Coaching Handbook, the companion book* to *Basketball Skill Progressions*, can prepare parent-coaches to coach and develop youngsters through the basketball-playing experience. It is designed to provide you with what you need to know about coaching youngsters, including:

- Reasons for coaching
- Developing a coaching philosophy
- Motivating young athletes
- Planning/organization
- Game coaching
- Establishing personnel roles
- Developing essential skills
- Monitoring and controlling player behavior
- Developing character lessons

---

* The NABC offers an instructional package for youth basketball coaches that features two books—*Basketball Skill Progressions* and *NABC's Youth Basketball Coaching Handbook*.

- Teaching tips
- Coaching/parent checklists
- Coaching resources

With knowledge of, and experience in, both technical basketball and the development of young people, you can feel confident that players entrusted to your care will have worthwhile experiences and you will have earned the title of "coach." Best wishes on your journey. The coauthors have compiled the results of more than 80 years of collective coaching experience to bring this information to you.

1

Overview

"A good game requires good players first, then good officials and good coaches."
—C.M. Newton, Naismith Hall of Fame Basketball Coach

It has been said that a good game in sports depends upon good players, good officials, and good coaches. The individuals who organize and administer youth sport programs could also be added to that list. Players are always the key ingredient—sports like basketball should always begin (and end) with a focus on the people playing the game. In youth basketball, the sport is really a means to the end goal of developing the youngsters who play the game. The sport of basketball is just an avenue—hopefully an enjoyable and worthwhile one—that can be used to help young people develop in many ways.

Good officials can, through their love of the game, also assist in developing young people. They help establish the boundaries of the game and teach kids the rules of basketball. Also, by carrying out their role, officials can help players develop respect for themselves, for authority figures, and for the game itself.

The final, and possibly the most critical, piece to the puzzle of educational sports are the coaches (and probably the administrators) who lead and teach the game of basketball. They are the "difference makers" in determining the value of the sport experience. So, if you are a former athlete who loves basketball, a trained coach, or an interested parent who wants kids to be involved in a worthwhile experience, you

Good game—good coaches and good players

should consider becoming a youth basketball coach, or at least become someone who can evaluate and recognize good basketball programs. Your goals should include ensuring that all young people participate in basketball programs that are appropriate for them, and are the "best programs they can be."

Reasons for Coaching

Making the decision to coach should be done with care. Coaching first requires a love of kids and a strong *determination* (not just a desire) to help provide a worthwhile sport experience for *all* the kids you coach. You must have a genuine love of young people and a consuming desire to develop them. Then, and only then, should you consider the second basic criteria, which is your interest in, and knowledge of, basketball. In essence, the two best reasons for wanting to coach youth basketball are as follows:

- Love of kids and a desire to educate them through basketball
- Interest in, and knowledge of, the sport of basketball

Note the order and relative importance of these two coaching criteria. You need to know how to coach kids first (using basketball as an educational/developmental tool), and then be able to coach basketball. You may have other reasons to coach that work for you, but these criteria are paramount for good basketball and worthwhile sport experiences for the young people who play the game. The most important thing to understand is that coaches don't coach basketball. They coach young people through the sport of basketball.

The Qualities of a Successful Coach

The qualities of a successful youth basketball coach go hand in hand with the valid reasons for wanting to coach. Youth coaches need to be able to help players develop physically (both as a skilled player and as a better, more fit, conditioned person), mentally (both psychologically and emotionally), and socially (through learning to play on a team). This quality will depend more on your understanding of young people than your knowledge of basketball, although that is also important. Physical development is essential, because it provides the movement and basketball skill base that enables players to enjoy success and learn to love the sport. The other part of facilitating physical development is providing a fun environment that assists youngsters in the development of active, healthy lifestyles through the enjoyment of sports. The high rates of inactivity and obesity in children certainly point out the need for active lifestyle habits. Basketball, which is easily adaptable to various skill and fitness levels, can certainly be part of a long-term solution.

Coaching—must love youngsters

Morgan Wootten, the legendary Hall of Fame basketball coach who spent most of his career at DeMatha High School in Hyattsville, MD, became known for fostering the growth and development of the players he coached. Wootten stated that the measure of any coach is determined by the kind of person their players later become. His coaching philosophy is summarized in his statement that he wanted his players to "play hard, play smart, play together, and have fun." What valuable lessons these are!

Some of the qualities needed to accomplish such lofty coaching goals are leadership; understanding of, and empathy for, young people; a sound coaching philosophy; teaching/educating skills; communication/motivation skills; planning skills (organizational and administrative); and basketball knowledge (rules, fundamental skills, tactics, and strategy). The greatest of these qualities is the leadership that you must possess as a coach. Leadership is a trait that you inherit as a person, but can develop around your own personality. Learning to lead is an indispensable asset in working with youngsters.

Stand Up and Be Counted

Whether you decide to become involved in coaching (or administering) a program of youth basketball, or you are a parent who simply knows what a good sport experience should be and want to assist coaching your own child in having that worthwhile basketball experience, you can benefit from the information and insights presented in this book and its companion text, *Basketball Skill Progressions*, as well as the rest of the NABC Youth Basketball packet. Whatever your role, you should carefully consider your place in the sport experiences of children. The "difference makers" that determine the worth of youth basketball are parents, coaches, and administrators who are focused on doing what is best for the total development of all children through basketball. It is your responsibility to "stand up and be counted" as a positive person who helps develop beneficial sport experiences for all youngsters. Select one of these roles—and only one—and learn to do it to the best of your ability.

Coaches—develop young players

2

Philosophy

"Youth basketball should focus on fun and fundamentals."

—Jerry Krause, Hall of Fame Coach

Coach/Program Philosophy

Your personal philosophy, along with the overall philosophy of your youth basketball program, will in many ways determine the worth of the program and your effect on the players. Program administrators may determine the overall philosophy, but, at the player level, your philosophy strongly influences the quality of the players' experiences.

The National Association of Basketball Coaches (NABC), the preeminent basketball coaching organization in the United States, has stated its organizational philosophy in the NABC motto—"Guardians of the Game." As an organization, the NABC is responsible for promoting and protecting the integrity and the positive development of basketball. This philosophy, when applied to youth basketball, means that the coaches, administrators, and parents most responsible for youth programs need to develop a sound philosophy that allows youngsters to develop through worthwhile basketball experiences and learn to love the game. The "guardians of the game" of basketball are strongly supportive of youth basketball programs that have a sound philosophy that keeps winning in perspective, allows kids to develop in all ways, and fosters a love for the game.

All players need success

What is philosophy? *Webster's Dictionary* describes it as the general principles underlying an area of knowledge. Therefore, a coaching philosophy encompasses your ideas about coaching a sport. The "practical wisdom" you state in your coaching philosophy should turn your coaching ideas into action.

Many former basketball players and coaches grew up in a time when sports were informal, recreational, and controlled by kids. Some people feel that the development of a love for the game is enhanced by informal play that is organized and administered by the players. In other words, learning to love basketball as a worthwhile activity is best accomplished when young people organize, coach, officiate, and play the sport themselves and have fun as they learn to play the game.

This scenario is a far cry from how most kids learn to play basketball—organized leagues, overzealous (and sometimes misinformed and untrained) coaches, overinvolved parents, ambitious officials, and an overemphasis on competition and winning. That is not a pretty picture of youth basketball at its beginning levels.

Therefore, a need was identified for a sound basketball guide for coaches and parents of younger players. This book teaches you how to organize and plan effective practice/play sessions and how to make the necessary age-appropriate modifications for optimal learning. Finally a sequential, progressive approach to youth basketball that is developmentally appropriate for all age levels is presented. You will find the information you need to prepare for basketball coaching or to evaluate a youth basketball program. The skills that you should teach young players and guidelines for when they should be taught are provided in *Basketball Skill Progressions*.

When examining the world of sports in the twenty-first century, you will find a real dichotomy. "Business/entertainment sports" can be contrasted with "educational sports." The concept of educational sports focuses on the development of the athlete or, more correctly, the development of the whole person who is playing the sport. In this framework, basketball is a medium for educating the person as a means to that end. Most sport decisions in educational sports are made with the players' welfare as the prime concern. For example, players can be encouraged to "call their own fouls" (i.e., self-officiate), which forces them to take responsibility for their actions and develop the habit of "doing the right thing." Peer pressure thereby influences the development of honesty. Basketball in this format is more focused on education and development of the physical, emotional, and social aspects of the game. Playing for fun and the love of the game is the primary focus.

At the other end of the sports continuum is the "play for pay" emphasis (i.e., business/entertainment sports). In this format, winning is paramount and success is most often defined in terms of winning and/or the accumulation of money. This type of environment is exemplified by professional sports and to some extent college and high school sports. Certainly, sports are hardly ever strictly "educational" or strictly "business," but they operate somewhere along the sports continuum shown in Figure 2-1.

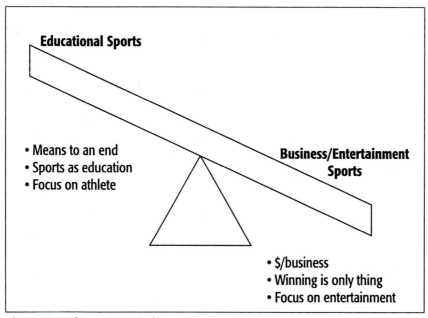

Figure 2-1. The sports continuum

When discussing youth basketball from preschool to K-12 school programs, it is important to consider what would be the best experience for young people in each of those basketball settings. It is strongly recommended that the philosophy of basketball be geared toward the educational sports end of the continuum. The philosophical foundation of "athletes first, winning second" is essential, as advocated by the American Sport Education Program (ASEP). This philosophy is an example of youth sports focused on the needs of the beginning athlete. But why is this type of philosophy essential?

Players believe that the most important thing in sport is having fun, even though they generally believe that winning is also important. Joe Paterno, the Penn State football coach who is one of the winningest coaches of all time has said, "We can't let people make kids think they've got to win. The winning is great. You strive for it. You try to do it. You compete to win. But if we lose, we lose. I've never been in a football game where there wasn't enough glory for everybody—winners and losers."

According to a *USA Today* survey of youth sports participants, more than 75% of kids who started playing sports at age six or seven have quit by the age of 15. The primary reason listed was because it wasn't fun anymore. Therefore, the primary focus of youth basketball should be rooted in teaching the fundamentals of the game while making it fun as well.

Fun and Fundamentals

It is important to apply an educational sports philosophy like "athletes first, winning second" by concentrating on developing kids through basketball in a setting where the sport is perceived as fun. This approach consists of teaching the fundamental basketball skills, including footwork (stance and steps), ballhandling (dribbling, passing, and catching), shooting, rebounding, and individual defense. This environment can be created through a variety of teaching methods, including the games approach (see Appendix D). Children sometimes perceive this experience as hard work, but mastering these skills can lead to delight. A sense of accomplishment is gained through achieving worthwhile skill goals and, eventually, fun and self-confidence is derived from worthwhile challenges that are met and mastered.

Success for All

It is also important to develop a definition of success that is achievable by each player and is not necessarily related to winning. The best definition from the basketball world comes from John Wooden, the legendary former UCLA coach. His definition allows each child the chance to succeed and have fun through that achievement. Wooden

Teach fun and fundamentals

states, "Success is peace of mind that is a direct result of self-satisfaction in knowing you did your best to become the best you are capable of becoming." Success in youth basketball should be centered on individuals doing their best, a goal that every participant can reach in an "educational sports" basketball experience.

Your Coaching Philosophy

With a "fun and fundamentals" focus and "success for all" as a goal, every youth basketball coach can develop his own unique coaching philosophy. By doing so, every coach has a core coaching philosophy based upon the solid foundation of worthy concepts, such as:

- Empowerment—basketball programs should center on youngsters and their needs
- Athletes first, winning second—keep winning in perspective as the athletes are developed physically, emotionally, and socially
- NABC Guardians of the Game—make programs worthwhile and enjoyable as youngsters are taught to love basketball
- Fun and fundamentals—combine the two to create the ideal youth basketball program
- Success for all—everyone learns and everyone plays
- The coaches unique personality—used as a *basis* for leading, motivating, teaching, and mentoring
- Technical basketball suited to the motivation level of your team
- Self-worth developed in *every* player

Note that most often, players gauge their self-worth by whether they win or lose. You need to change this measure of success and instead focus on personal goals. Athletes must see success in terms of achieving their own goals in a team framework, which is a cardinal rule for motivation (see Chapter 3).

Many examples of alternative sport philosophies exist for youth sports that do not subscribe to the business/entertainment (winning is everything) sports model. One such example in youth football is described in *Season of Life* by Jeffery Marx. This book is about Joe Ehrmann, a former NFL star who has developed a philosophy centered on teaching boys how to become men—he calls the philosophy Building Men for Others. At Gilman School in Baltimore, where Ehrmann coaches, the sport philosophy is:

- Allow yourself to love and be loved. Build and value relationships.
- Accept responsibility, lead courageously, and enact justice on behalf of others.
- Practice the concepts of empathy, inclusion, and integrity.
- Learn the importance of serving others. Base your thoughts and actions on the question, "What can I do for you?"
- Develop a cause beyond yourself. Try to leave the world a better place because you were here.

Ehrmann states that such a philosophy forces players to recognize the three lies of false masculinity—athletic ability, sexual conquest, and economic success as measures of manhood. Instead, sports are about living in a community and building relationships with friends who care. Coaches must never shame players, but correct them in an uplifting and loving way. The senior tradition at Gilman is to have each graduating player write and share an essay entitled, "How I Want to be Remembered When I Die," to express how this sports philosophy and experience has impacted him.

Encourage young athletes to do the following in your efforts to create a coaching/program philosophy:

- Replace individual celebration rituals with ones that promote team solidarity. The message is that togetherness is more solemn and fun than any passing victory.
- Tell them to "discover themselves" while playing sports. Sport can allow a person to make a self. The message to players is, work hard and put your fate in your own hands.
- Great teacher/coaches demystify the sport experience. They give students or athletes the subject matter and then offer themselves as exemplary leaders. In this way, anyone can follow, anyone can see, and anyone can develop themselves.

The challenge is now yours. Use Checklist #1 in Appendix A to develop your own written philosophy of coaching youth basketball, and you will be on your way.

3

Motivation

"The strength of the group is in the strength of the leaders."

—Vince Lombardi, Hall of Fame Football Coach

Overview—What Does Motivation Look Like?

The purpose of this chapter is to describe attributes that develop a coaching style that produces motivated athletes and teams, propels players into action, and activates the hearts, minds, and behaviors of your players. A coach with these attributes understands that motivation is much more than the verbal pregame or halftime "pep talk" that many people recognize as "motivation."

Motivation is defined as a force that propels people into action. It is the "motive to act," an inner drive. What kind of "action" do you want your coaching to inspire? In sport, as in life, either the hope of achieving a particular result or a fear of experiencing a specific consequence triggers most internal motivation. The ultimate goal of motivation, though, is to get people to perform up to their capabilities and enjoy doing it. Leaders who understand and produce a motivating environment get people to achieve beyond their own perceived limits.

It is a fact that fear works as a motivator (to a degree), but individuals motivated by fear not only get discouraged more easily, but also can become resentful of the leader who is imposing the fear. On teams where fear is used as the primary form of motivation and punishment is always given for mistakes, players will tend to avoid taking on any responsibility to prevent making mistakes and receiving the anticipated punishment. Fear does not function nearly as well as love and respect, which bring a deeper purpose to the individual's motivation. A team motivated through love and respect produces great memories and lasting friendships. Tasks are completed, discipline accepted, and expectations increased, because teammates do not want to let each other down. They depend on and trust one another to complete their mission. Each role tends to become equal in value on a team where individuals value each other. Teams built around love, respect, and group responsibility lean on each other in times of trouble and tend to be able to successfully sustain their motivation for longer periods of time.

Motivating through fear may work in the short term to get people to do something, but over the long run I believe personal pride is a much greater motivator. It produces far better results that last for a much longer time.

—John Wooden, Naismith Hall of Fame Player and Coach

Coaching and Motivation

The ability to motivate is one of the key differences between good coaches and great coaches. Good coaches can encourage and motivate. Great coaches motivate through love and get every ounce of attention and energy from their athletes.

The responsibility for providing motivation (especially for younger players) falls directly on the shoulders of the coach. As a coach, you have the ability to make your athletes feel comfortable, energized, focused, and excited. Some people have a natural gift to motivate people, but everyone can learn to be a better motivator.

The concept of *motivational coaching* is simple. Decide what is important to you as the coach and for the team, and then find a way to make the same things important to the players. The ultimate purpose is to get players to play better and to perform with their peak attention, effort, and behavior levels.

> *Is offensive rebounding important to you? Then find a way to make it important to the players. Is diving on the floor for loose ball important to you? Being a great defensive team? Having a great attitude? Being a focused and motivated team? It is up to you to help players see the same vision that you see.*

Coaches who successfully motivate players have learned how to:
- Take a negative and turn it into a positive
- Keep a positive string going
- Reach all kinds of athletic personalities
- Avoid the pitfalls of defeatism
- Use their personality and the natural influence of coaching to effectively and consistently activate players and assistant coaches

Think of people who you like to spend time with. What is it about them that is so appealing? Normally, it is people who love what they do and where they are, and let it show. Be a coach who celebrates small successes and avoids complaining and making excuses. Develop a style that builds everything and everyone up.

One of a coach's primary jobs is to motivate, which requires energy and an investment in each athlete in an effort to create the ultimate motivated group. Inspiration and motivation are ongoing responsibilities that will not be completed during a season. Coaches are the key to motivated teams. Create a climate for success and become a coach who is motivated and can motivate others.

Coaching Motivation Concepts

> *"Knowledge alone is not enough to get desired results. You must have the more elusive ability to teach and motivate. This defines a leader."*
>
> —John Wooden, Naismith Hall of Fame Player and Coach

Keep Motivation Simple

Remember that fun is at the heart of almost every motivated player, and having fun produces positive attitudes. Being recognized for doing something well is all that is needed for most athletes to have fun. Fun is the best reward an athlete can experience.

Motivated players have fun and learn fundamentals

Define Having Fun as Being Good

As athletes mature, they go from defining fun as "being silly" to defining it as "being good"—good workers; accomplished performers; focused, attentive listeners; and accountable, trusted teammates. An important step of maturity for any young athlete is to grow beyond the age of silliness into becoming an athlete who enjoys the work, effort, and skills necessary to be competitive.

Focus on Things Over Which You Have Control

As a coach, you must use your energy and expertise to focus only on areas that you can control—preparation, attitude, effort, and behavior. Take full advantage of the areas where you have control and become a positive motivating force. Develop a sense of urgency and do not waste your time and energy on matters that are beyond your control or are not essential for team success. Trying to influence the areas of the game over which you have no control will frustrate you and your players, and will get your focus off the important areas. Focus positively and aggressively on factors that are controllable and do not worry about the others.

Control	No Control
Effort of your team	*Ability or size of your opponents*
Behavior of your team	*Behavior of the opponents*
Preparation of your team	*Officials' decisions*
Motivation level of your team	*Coaching decisions made by the*
Your in-game coaching decisions	*opposing coach*
	Fans' behavior

Learn to be "Positive Demanding"

One of the best terms for motivational leadership in athletics is "positive demanding." Coaches who possess this attribute are relaxed and confident, while maintaining a naturally competitive personality. They have learned to teach and coach while maintaining the delicate balance between fun and discipline. Discipline and fun need each other to maintain their effectiveness. Only having fun becomes an unproductive waste of time and energy, while focusing only on discipline creates an environment of forced labor. A sense of fun is necessary to sustain effort and keep things in perspective. Put fun into your practices by enjoying them yourself. Let your enjoyment show. A sense of discipline is necessary, of course, because all athletes and teams need to be able to focus. Discipline in athletics is simply focused attention and effort.

Positive demanding coaching

Think back to the best teacher you ever had. He was probably both "tough" and "nice." He likely expected your best effort and made you work, but you liked and respected him. If a coach is demanding out of love and respect, he will get all kinds of results. However, once a coach's words and actions become demeaning, the athlete puts up wall of resistance, trust is broken, and learning stops. If you are demanding and use fear as a motivational tool, your athletes will probably respond, but they will compete fearfully. *Coaches are either confidence builders or confidence cutters.* Confidence builders deal honestly and directly with mistakes, but are always able to recognize when people are doing things well and always reinforce that behavior. Focus on what athletes *can do*, rather on what they cannot do. Positive-demanding coaches work to have their athletes improve their weaknesses, while constantly stressing their strengths. They also have a style that establishes a tone in practices of expecting and accepting only all-out effort. They demand and receive the best from each team member.

Teach Athletes That Small Successes Lead to Large Successes

Find and celebrate small successes. Build a foundation upon small successes in practice. Find "victories" in every way that you can, even if it means that you must "set them up" in practice. Begin with small successes rather than create frustration by setting goals that are too high. Once your players see that they can succeed in small ways, their personal and team vision will expand. People who are willing to take on large and demanding challenges are those who have experienced small successes along the way.

Use Punishment Sparingly

Punishment is acceptable when it is used to change behaviors that cannot be changed with positive reinforcement. It can also be used when a player interferes with his teammates' ability and right to learn or with your right and ability to teach. Be prepared to confront any behavior that is not acceptable to the team's core covenants.

Punishment works, and it has a place in a coach's method of motivating people to action. Punishment has to be practiced sparingly, though, especially when compared to the amount of energy used to positively motivate, and it should be used in conjunction with positive reinforcement.

Punishment can create more problems if used incorrectly or too often. When used correctly, punishment can be an effective form of behavior modification. Carefully evaluate your approach to punishment. Does the punishment simply suppress the behavior, or does it change it? If the athlete who was punished continually finds himself in the same situation, he hasn't learned what is expected and accepted. In a follow-up conversation with the athlete, explain alternative choices to replace the unacceptable behaviors.

If you discover that punishment is your main source of control, it will quickly lose it effectiveness. You will have to be ready to use it more and more until it becomes part of your style and of the athletes' expectations. Not only is this an unproductive use of your teaching time, but it also takes away the positive energy that you give to athletes making good choices. *Your energy is always better spent in the pursuit of positive reinforcement*. Rewarding positive behavior also tells athletes that you want the action repeated. Use punishment to respond to behaviors that are infrequent, disruptive, or disrespectful violations of what the team stands for.

How to Administer Punishment

When administering punishment, be as impersonal as possible. Correct the behavior or action, *not the person*. Be consistent, but flexible enough to help in each individual situation. Do not continually threaten action; instead, just follow through. Times will come when you need time to calm down or think of what is appropriate before acting. In such situations, tell the athlete to sit down and that you will talk to him in a few minutes. But do not wait too long to confront the behavior. The sooner you handle the situation, the better the chance for change.

It is also important that you keep your conversations, descriptions, and actions with players short and to the point. Be as clear as possible about the unacceptable behavior. Instead of addressing generic behaviors (e.g., "you have a bad attitude"), identify the specific behavior. Your corrective discipline will be much more effective if you can specify the violation.

Examples of identifying specific behaviors:
- *Your use of profanity is not acceptable at any time on this team.*
- *Your level of effort and attention is not acceptable.*
- *The way you reacted when you were called for a foul was not acceptable behavior on this team. Have a seat over there and I will talk to you when I get a break in practice.*

Use quick, concise sentences to get the exact point across and do not disrupt the pace of practice or give the unwanted behavior any more attention than it deserves. Quickly turn your positive energy and focus back to the group that was doing things correctly in the first place and use positive praise. Hearing others being praised for correct actions while not hearing his own name sends a player an important message.

Times will arise when the best response is to ignore the behavior. Not rewarding a behavior with any of your attention will normally cause the player to stop the action. If a player is acting out with the intention of getting your attention, don't give him any. This technique requires patience and forethought. Sometimes a coach's reaction to situations actually brings the wanted attention to the misbehavior and encourages the offender to repeat it. Ignoring the behavior teaches players that it is not worthy of your attention or worth getting upset over. If you believe that the best response is to ignore the misbehavior, do it as long as possible and then take action. Because every person has different levels of tolerance, it is impossible to identify the exact point where you should go from ignoring the behavior to confronting it. In general, confront problems early in the season with a low level of tolerance, and use punishment more sparingly as you move through the season.

Another way of "ignoring" a player is through isolation, which may be the best form of punishment for many young players. Isolation removes a player from the team, the situation, and the attention for a specific time period (e.g., five minutes, one drill, until you have a break in practice, for the remainder of practice, for a week, for a season). Isolation eliminates the player being punished from receiving the best things about practices—the fun and your positive attention and reinforcement.

Do not punish players for physical errors—this response produces fearful play. Never use running as punishment in sports in which being in peak condition is essential for success. Think about it this way: You tell your athletes how important it is to team success that they are in peak condition and then you tell them to run when you're upset with them. This technique equates physical fitness with punishment. (See *Teaching Character Through Sport: Developing a Positive Coaching Legacy* by Bruce Brown, Chapter 10: Team Building Through Positive Conditioning.)

Use Mistakes to Build a Level of Trust

In athletics, mistakes are an essential part of the growth process. You are constantly asking your players to learn new concepts, strategies, and skills. New learning does not happen without some failure. No matter how or when mistakes are made, they are usually difficult for the player and coach, who are both hoping for success. Every effort to demonstrate a new skill is an opportunity for failure—not just failure, but failure in front of teammates, coaches, and spectators. Teach your athletes how to fail, recover quickly, and try again. The faster they recover—and try again—the sooner they will master the skill. This kind of recovery requires either very strong self-confidence or trust of the person who is asking him to risk failure. Trust at moments like this is based upon how you respond verbally and physically to the mistake. Coaches who can motivate their players through mistakes are the ones who have learned how to separate mistakes made because of carelessness, lack of attention, or lack of effort from mistakes made with the athlete's best effort. Such coaches have learned to dignify with actions and words all those mistakes made at full speed and with full attention.

Teams and individual players who trust their coach will listen, fail, recover, improve, and be able to play fearlessly. Players who are fearful of the coach's reaction to a mistake play to not make a mistake and, therefore compete fearfully.

Use Roles to Motivate—All Roles Have Equal Value

One of the fundamental responsibilities of successful team leadership is to eliminate selfishness. Selfishness on the team level or with any individual player will destroy the team faster than anything else. A "team first" attitude will allow people to accept roles that make others better. Great teams have individual players who each make their own unique contribution to the group's success. Players should be expected to be unselfish with their efforts and unselfish when playing their roles. Every decision should be based on the question, "What does the team need from me?"

Every successful team must have people willing to do a variety of things. The following roles are like "job descriptions," in that the players can decide how they can best help the team. It is important to place equal value on all roles (e.g., the player who sets the screen is just as important as the player who comes off the screen and makes the shot). Also, it is a good idea to have players talk to the coach about the roles they think they can play and the roles that they would like to "grow into."

Consider a player who says, "I know that right now I can fill the role of a screener and rebounder, but I would like to become a defensive stopper and an interior scorer." He has just declared his current value to the team and has also opened himself up to be coached in the areas he wants to grow into.

No one player has to do everything, but filling each of these jobs with at least players will allow for a better chance for group success:
- Defensive stopper—A player who can take the other team's best offensive player and shut him down
- Passer—A person who thinks pass first and understands where the ball needs to be moved
- Decision-maker—The player who usually handles the ball on the fast break or to initiate the offense and the player who you want to have the ball when an offensive set has to be run correctly
- Rebounder—A disciplined player who understands that rebounds usually go to the most determined players, especially offensive rebounds

- Screener—A person who is willing to get his teammates open with solid screens
- Encourager—A player who is always looking to encourage others, whether he is in the game or on the bench
- Perimeter scorer—A player who has the green light to shoot the ball from the outside
- Interior scorer—A player who can draw fouls or score from the block (post players)
- Leader—A player who leads the way in every practice and game and who is connected with the coach and can become his voice on the floor
- Follower—A player who can listen and follow the player in the leadership position

Motivate through fun and success

Although some roles appear to have more importance than others, it is the combination of skills (i.e., roles) that allows a team to reach its ultimate potential. Roles give players their identities. Every team member can bring a different strength to the big picture. Clarification and specification of roles aids in the acceptance of those roles and the performance of each individual. An understanding of all the roles must be shared to be effective. When each member understands his own role(s), as well as the roles of his teammates, he will be much more productive and will feel able to participate to his fullest potential. As a result, a "team identity" will begin to be formed.

When you give each role equal value in the eyes of the team, your leadership is more readily accepted and appreciated. Too often, the perception is that the coach only focuses on the "high-profile" roles of the player who scores the most points. It is obvious to everyone who watches a game that the people who score are important, and therefore they receive the most attention. But, if it were not for the player who made the pass to the scorer, or the player who set the screen to free up the scorer, the team would not have succeeded in scoring.

Roles can either be a force that binds the team together or creates jealousy among the individual players. If value is shown equally to every role, it is easier for each role to be embraced by every player. The more each individual squad member feels like he is part of the team, the more he will contribute. And the more each member contributes, the more he feels like part of the team and the overall success that the team achieves. Players will form an identity within the team for the positive roles they fulfill and, in turn, will relish their roles even more.

Practices vs. Games

Players who do not attend practice should not play in games. One of the biggest problems in youth sports is that games have taken on more importance and practices have been given less importance. Too often, young people (and even their parents) look at games as the only valuable part of the athletic experience. The exact opposite should be true. Players will be well served to learn that practices are equal to, if not more important than, games, and that productive practices are fun. Too many young people have learned that being an "athlete" means putting on pro-style adult uniforms, playing 40 games, and having 10 practices during a three-month season. More things can and should be gained from practicing that enhance the athletic experience far more than games do. Young athletes should practice much more than they play, thereby learning skills as well as work habits and discipline. Too many youth "coaches" are simply managers who organize players and put them in positions to play in games, rather than prepare for practice and teach the skills needed to improve. Games are important and allow for growth, but well-organized, instructionally based, highly motivating practices should be the best part of a season.

Practice Motivation

One of the best ways to ensure a motivated team is a well-organized practice. Similarly, one of the quickest ways to lose motivation is to conduct a poorly planned, disorganized practice.

You must be creative, but organized, at practice. The best teachers and coaches are creative craftsmen. They are people who have found a variety of methods to teach the same material. Coaches who can find a way to turn the routine into something exciting can keep players from becoming bored. You cannot be afraid to be different and should look for ways to keep your players energized. The following simple concepts can keep practices from becoming boring and will help you create a motivational learning environment.

Individual Competition vs. Collective Competition

To increase the level of motivation in practice, all you typically have to do is find a way to keep score. Make drills as competitive as possible, but only once they have been learned and when the players are attempting to improve through repetition. Competition is a natural energizer for most athletes. The natural competitiveness in athletes will increase when an activity is measured in any way. Without even declaring a "winner," keeping score raises the level of attention, energy, and effort. While it is easy to set up player-against-player competitions, what is energizing for the winning player will often become deflating for the one who loses. Individual competition is effective, but doesn't always bring about team unity. Think about adjusting the way you do a drill so that the players are competing together against a time or goal. It is not difficult to take any drill and have the players combine their efforts to reach a "team goal" and compete against a standard.

Instead of saying, "Let's see which player can make the most shots in the next minute," change the focus to a team goal by saying, "Let's see how many shots we can make as a team in the next minute," or, "Let's see how long it takes us to make 100 shots as a team." This format takes the focus off individual wins and losses and puts every player in a position where he can both contribute and "win." This concept can be applied to almost any competitive practice situation.

Varying the Type and Duration of Each Drill

Once the drills are learned and the team is working to improve through repetition, do not do the same routine in the same order every day. Another motivational concept is to shorten the time segments once the drills have been taught. Create a sense of urgency that you have limited time in practice to get better at this particular skill. Repetition is the key to motor learning, but the benefits of small doses repeated regularly at game speed and with maximum effort far exceed the benefit of the same work done for long periods of time with lesser form and concentration. Also, alternate physically demanding drills with ones that are less so.

For example, if you need to spend 20 minutes on a specific skill, consider breaking it down into two separate 10-minute sessions, or, even better, four five-minute sessions.

Practices Must Be Game-Like

Make your practices as game-like as possible. Prepare players for the toughest competition that they will face by working at game-speed and with a game-like mentality. Give your athletes the experience of being challenged and producing under the pressure situations they will face in the game. Structure practices so that players rehearse behaviors, skills, and decisions that they are familiar with and can be successful performing. Choose skills that are age-appropriate and possess the right balance of challenge and achievability.

Activity Levels

Keep your players' activity level up. Since one of the keys to improvement is repetition, drills should be active, with short lines and lots of repetitions. Working in small groups that are organized according to each player's level of expertise not only allows each athlete to progress at his own rate, but also gives each player more repetitions. Players learn by doing.

Coach at the Pace of the Quickest Learners

This may sound contrary to most educational beliefs, but one of the best ways to kill motivation in practice is to bore your stronger players. Teach at a pace at which your more advanced players are challenged. You must set the stage with players at all levels by letting them know that you will be willing to come early before practice or stay afterward and give extra help to those who didn't understand a particular skill. Do not expect skills to be mastered at the same rate by all players. You must understand how to help athletes who are struggling with the "basics" without boring those who are ready to practice more advanced skills.

Naming Drills After Players

One of the best ways to increase the level of performance during drills is to name the drill after the player in your coaching past who performed that drill the best. Players will inevitably want a drill named after them. Any time you introduce a drill that you, as coach, have never used before, it can be claimed by the person who does it best that day.

Planning Your Practices

Come into every practice with a plan. Plan your practice so that drills that are new or require more thinking occur early in practice. Drills done at the end of practice should be the ones that require the proper execution of fundamentals while players are tired.

Establish the best possible learning environment for your team. Make the best out of whatever conditions you are assigned by doing the following:

- Think "positive practicing"—everything can be done better and all great efforts can be recognized and rewarded.
- Start on time, stay on time, and end on time.
- Once the team's expectations have been established, eliminate players who do not listen or try. Be willing to help them with their problem at another time, but the focus of practice cannot be lost due to behavioral problems.
- Talk less and show more. One of the most common coaching techniques that actually reduces motivation is having the athletes do too much listening. Coaches who try to describe everything to their players with words (e.g., how to do a skill) aren't taking advantage of the knowledge that most athletes are visual learners and action and correct repetition are what teach physical skills. Almost all coaches need to talk less and show more. Give players time away from your voice and instruction, time to be totally absorbed and focused on the activity. Avoid constantly evaluating athletes, especially during a game. Most corrections can be made one on one so the flow of practice is not interrupted. The only time everyone should have to listen to a correction is when it applies to every player.
- Understand that how much you know is not really that important. The important thing is how much of what you know you can effectively teach to the players so they can perform at their highest level. Keep the game simple and easy to learn.
- Make sure that every drill has a clearly defined purpose within the team concept. Athletes will learn a new skill more easily if they see it as meaningful and useful to the big picture.

Coaches who talk too much lose the most active of players. Keep your words and instructions concise. Use as few words as possible and let the players see the skill done correctly. Then give them more repetitions with quick individual corrections rather than allowing them to stand and listen as you talk. Use your words only to focus the attention on specific details. Follow the progression of accurate demonstration, practice, quick reinforcing correction, and more practice. John Wooden says the eight laws of learning are, "explanation, demonstration, imitation, repetition, repetition, repetition, repetition, repetition." Nothing in athletics should be taught using just words. Everything needs visual demonstration and lots of repetitions.

- Make sure that the drills are structured so that both you and the players can clearly discern improvement. Players will be more eager to learn when they feel that they are making progress in a drill and can see results from the drill carried over into games.
- Seek (on an ongoing basis) new drills and techniques for performing specific skills that can help your players improve. Focus on the skills, not the drills.
- Fully understand your teaching environment before you begin teaching a drill for the first time. For example, how many players do you have? How much space? How many baskets? How much time? How many coaches? How can you maximize all these variables?
- Teach correctly the *first time* to maximize the learning environment for a drill. You need to plan and prepare so that you use the correct technique and correct terminology the first time a skill is introduced. Having to correct things that are taught poorly or incorrectly requires "unteaching" and "reteaching," which take time and confuse the athletes.
- Allow adequate time for making corrections when drills or techniques are improperly performed.
- Demonstrate (or have someone else demonstrate) the whole picture of the drill, break the drill down into teachable parts, and then build it back to the whole.
- Emphasize the parts of the drill done correctly at increasing levels of speed as the skill level of the players improves.
- Attempt to end every practice on a fun note. Athletes should leave practice wishing it wasn't over and eager for the next practice to begin. When players leave practice they should be energized to go home and work on the skills that they are learning or just go shoot baskets with a family member. It doesn't take much creativity to

find a way to leave them smiling. Refer to Chapter 9 in *101 Youth Basketball Drills and Games* or the *Fun Ways to End Basketball Practice* video, both by Bruce Brown.

- Be willing to come early and stay after practice to assist any player who wants extra help.

Rewarding Statistics—Stats That Matter

Using Statistics to Motivate

Another basic principle of motivation states that whatever you measure is more likely to get done. Most coaches keep game statistics that consist of the basic numbers, including field goals attempted, field goals made, free throws attempted, free throws made, rebounds (possibly divided between offensive and defensive), assists, and turnovers. Those statistics are important for assessing the game and even for assessing individual athletes, but think about all the other areas of the game that are important to you as a coach. Remember the key concept behind coaching and motivation: Decide what is important to you and then make it important to your players. Coaches want their players to do certain things that help the team succeed and that can be measured while watching videotape. If it is important to you that your players dive on the floor for loose balls, then keep track of the number of times that they do so. Is it important to you that your players set solid screens? Then assess solid screens from the videotape and post that statistic.

It is easy to think of many areas of the game that could be called "team points," which go well beyond field goals and free throws. The following statistics can be kept once you've assigned them each a point value. These statistics will motivate players to do things that help the team.

Defense

- Stopping a drive by yourself and not requiring help (+1)
- Helping a teammate that got beat on a drive (+1)
- Getting a player with a dead dribble to turn his back to the basket (+2)
- Taking a charge on your man (+3)
- Taking a charge while helping a teammate (+4)
- Getting a deflection or any touch of the ball while on defense (+1)
- Getting a steal (+2)
- Grabbing a defensive rebound (+1)
- Making solid contact on a defensive block-out (+2)
- Diving on the floor for a loose ball (+2)

Offense

- Getting an assist (+1)
- Passing the ball to the post, who catches it (+1)
- Setting a screen that gets a teammate a shot (+1)
- Setting a screen for a teammate who makes the shot (+2) (if you want your players to screen for your better shooters)
- Diving on the floor for a loose ball (+2)
- Grabbing an offensive rebound (+3)
- Going hard to the offensive boards (+1) (not staying on an opponent's back, working to get inside position)

Identify the areas of the game that are important for your team to succeed and that you had focused on during practice, and then assign them positive team points. A player who sets, screens, stops his offensive player, dives on the floor, takes charges, keeps his opponent blocked-out on the defensive boards, and goes to the offensive boards hard is probably more important to the team than a player who shoots well from the field or free-throw line. These statistics encourage and reward the "small" things that win games and help the team. By identifying and rewarding these aspects of the game, you will likely find that player performance in these areas will improve dramatically. Players who could never score 20 points using the "normal" statistics will see the value you place on the important team points when statistics are posted and they see 32 points next to their names.

The same concept can be applied to any area of the game or even in practice. Practice statistics will give you an idea which of your players will be most likely to perform the same skills during a game.

Example: Offensive Rebounding

A simple identification and reward system that can be used to encourage offensive rebounding is to chart the number of times a player had the opportunity to go to the basket hard and the number of times that he actually did so. Establish criteria and describe it to the players so they understand which efforts will be counted and which will not. For an attempt to count, the player has to go early (immediately as the shot is taken), go hard (not be stopped by physical contact, but rather continue working or spinning to get around the opponent), or get inside position and hold it. Another factor that could be considered is if the player goes to the correct area of the floor based upon "rebound angles." After being assessed on videotape, each player has stats placed beside his name (e.g., seven for 12—or 58%—meaning that he had 12 opportunities to go to the offensive board and succeeded by meeting any of the criteria seven times). Players who understand exactly what you are looking for and realize that it can and will be accurately measured will find a way to perform this skill more effectively and more often. If you want your players to work on any particular skill, simply find a way to measure it and express it as a percentage.

Players	Stop Drib.	Help	Turn	Charge	Deflect	Floor	Blk Out	DR	TOTAL
Team Totals									

Figure 3-1. Example of a Defensive Team Points Statistical Sheet

Players	Assist	Screen	Off Reb	Off Reb Effort	Floor	Post Pass	Extra Effort	TOTAL
Team Totals								

Figure 3-2. Example of an Offensive Team Points Statistical Sheet

Motivating the Individual Athlete

Before thinking about how to motivate an individual athlete, it is important that you understand what kills motivation and the love of the game, so you can prevent those things from happening. The following five things, which are presented along with information regarding how much you can control each factor, can hurt natural motivation and destroy a young athlete's love of the game:

- Consistent defeats—you have some control (create successes in practice)
- Outside pressure (e.g., from parents)—you have little control (work with players on actions that assist performance; see Chapter 7)
- Mental or physical tiredness—you have quite a bit of control by what you do in practice

- Too much complexity in the game—you have complete control
- Negative coaching—you have complete control

Most young people are motivated to fulfill their own needs, so you must understand the needs of the age group you are working with and then help them reach those needs as often as possible. For most athletes, the primary sources of individual motivation are to have fun and feel worthy. A positive coaching style is the key to those two motivational sources.

To be capable of motivating the variety of individuals who make up a typical team, you must be *adjustable, flexible,* and *creative.* The enhancement of motivation requires different tactics in different situations. Individuals and teams present multiple situations and personalities, which also require different strategies and tactics. You must learn to fit your response and action to each situation. It is helpful to understand each player so that you know which buttons to push, who needs praise, who needs a push, who needs an aggressive approach, and who needs a calm style. After you choose your method of motivation, closely watch how each athlete performs to check the effectiveness of that approach. The more you know about each individual, the better chance you have to find the correct action for that person and situation.

Each moment and each player may require different motivational methods. Some people respond when you challenge them, while others only respond when you encourage them.

You are responsible for knowing how to reach individuals, as well as your team as a whole, for the team approach to be effective. You cannot expect them all to learn to deal with your style immediately. Most young people will adjust to you about as fast as you adjust to them. Learn as much as possible about the emotional and mental makeup of each player, as well as how they prefer to learn. Some players will respond to written material, while others prefer others only verbal directions. Some players even respond primarily to your body language. Your approach and words need to be appropriate not only for the situation, but also for the age of your athletes. You must learn what response fits which situation and person and then devise the correct reaction. Be aware and careful with each player to know when you may have gone too far. No motivational outcome is worth breaking someone's spirit and natural love for the game. Finding just the right words and the correct approach for each person and situation is almost impossible, but it is worth the effort. Get them to do all they are capable of and then allow them to enjoy themselves. Live the moment, the game, and the entire season along with them.

Motivating the Team

Motivation has to be looked at both individually and as a team. The best form of motivation in sports is based on the feeling of interdependence that comes with being part of a great team. Each player's best effort and focus is needed so the level of team motivation is unquestioned. Team performance is a collection of individually motivated players. On great teams, a collective power exists. These teams are usually competitive on the scoreboard, but it is not primarily the scoreboard that motivates them. They are motivated for each other and are unified by a pervasive feeling of, "I don't want to let my teammates down."

Within the team itself, a common agreement should exist concerning expectations for the team—and those expectations must be high. Great teams can figuratively "start their own engine" by allowing their collective personal motivation to strengthen and build each other. All factors considered, the clearer the mission and focus is within the team, the easier it is for team members to be motivated toward a united purpose. High morale magnifies all the positives that a team experiences. You should keep in mind that teams will seldom exceed the shared expectations or level of motivation of the group.

Motivated teams work in an atmosphere of openness. They are not afraid to hustle, to try, to ask for help, or even to fail in front of each other. They are bound together by the same love and respect their leader has for them. Love of team, the sport, and the sense of competition binds them together.

If you are ever part of a team built on interdependent motivation, you will discover that such teams:
- Produce friendships
- Reinforce and motivate each other
- Become dedicated to each other and don't want to let each other down
- Depend on and trust one another in good times and bad
- Sustain their individual and collective motivation for longer periods of time
- Value and accept roles more easily
- Have a common agreement on high expectations for the team
- Have a collective desire to succeed

When a strong desire to succeed exists among the team leaders, it is almost always spread in a positive manner until it impacts the entire group. The levels of commitment, achievement, unselfishness, energy, and confidence all expand. Motivated teams are competitive. Competition should exist for every position and role within the team. That competitive nature is appreciated by the best of teams and is seen as a viable means to improve the team's overall performance. Within that context, players on great teams band together to take the competitive nature that exists within the team to employ it against each and every opponent. They look forward to the toughest of competition and focus their preparation toward those moments. Teams built on a feeling of oneness and interdependence find that the strength of the team comes from a feeling of unity, not individualism.

Be the Coach for Whom You Would Have Liked to Play

What kind of coach would you like to play for? Normally, coaches who are happy, positive, knowledgeable, and demanding in a way that is never demeaning will inspire people. Analyze your reasons for coaching. What is your motivation to coach? What is driving your heart? Coaches of significance are leaders who are not in it for themselves but for the good of those they lead. Coach and teach with the idea of being a positive influence on each of the young people in your care. The key to true leadership is the leader's heart.

If you do not possess the natural gift of motivation, you can work, study, prepare, and improve, but in the meantime, surround yourself with people who have the gift and learn to coordinate your strengths. Your success or failure as a coach will be in direct proportion to your ability to plan, teach, relate, and motivate.

Great coaches view coaching as a "ministry," not a "part-time job." Making coaching a ministry gives more urgency to every minute you spend with young people, and gives purpose to the strategies you employ. Viewing coaching as an opportunity to motivate your athletes to the highest possible individual and team standards gives this profession eternal value.

4

Planning

"Failing to plan is planning to fail."
—John Wooden, Naismith Hall of Fame Player and Coach

Preplanning in youth basketball is important for both the players and the coach. Developing youngsters need the boundaries that proper planning provides, both in basketball and in life. Having a plan will optimize the chances for worthwhile experiences and basketball success. Likewise, you will benefit from the structure provided by planning to become a more confident coach who leads in an organized way and is as efficient as possible in the little time that is available for practice, games, and contact with players.

Planning consists of organization and administration. Organizational planning entails providing a structure or framework for the youth basketball program, including overall coaching, practices, games, equipment, facilities, supervision, knowledge of rules, player safety, and team strategies. Administration entails carrying out these plans in an effective and efficient way.

Season Plans

A brief season plan should provide an organized structure, which will give each coach and parent an overview of the basketball season. It can also be used as an outline of

Planning is organizing and administering

what a parent can expect from the sport experience for their child. A season plan should include the following:

- Program/coaching philosophy—a reminder of the focus on fun and fundamentals
- Parent letter and/or meeting covering the following:
  - ✓ Philosophy
  - ✓ Coach and player expectations
  - ✓ Goals and objectives
  - ✓ Solicitation for help (e.g., with transportation, equipment/facilities, and communication using a telephone/e-mail communication tree)
- Season/practice overview that includes the following fundamentals:
  - ✓ Footwork
  - ✓ Shooting (lay-ups, set/jump shots, free throws)
  - ✓ Ballhandling (passing, catching, dribbling)
  - ✓ Rebounding
  - ✓ Defense

- ✓ Setting and using screens
- ✓ Moving without the ball
- ✓ In addition, the following team strategies should be decided upon:
  - ○ Offense
  - ○ Defense
  - ○ Transitional play (especially from offense to defense, but also vice versa)
  - ○ Special situations (free throws, out-of-bounds plays, jump balls)
- A plan for teaching core values and basketball rules—for example, a basketball rule could be taught at each practice and a value such as "respect" could be stressed as the theme of the day
- Practice plan format   (For complete information on practice planning, see *Basketball Skill Progressions* and the video *NABC Basketball Skills & Drills for Younger Players: Volume 13—Practicing to Play the Game*, by Jerry Krause). The practice plan should include the following:
  - ✓ Theme of the day
  - ✓ Rule of the day
  - ✓ Equipment needed
  - ✓ Time allotments for practice areas
    - ○ Meet and greet
    - ○ Warm-up
    - ○ Fundamentals and fast breaks
    - ○ Team tactics (offense, defense, transition, special situations)
    - ○ Cool-down
    - ○ Meet and homework/reminders.
- Adjustments—the game (practicing and playing) should be adjusted to match the age and motivation level of the players on your team. These adjustments must be accomplished with input from the league or organizing groups (see *Basketball Skill Progressions*). Areas to be addressed include the following:
  - ✓ Participation (playing time, age, height)
  - ✓ Skill adjustments (individual and team)
  - ✓ Safety
  - ✓ Playing area

✓ Contest length

✓ Equipment

✓ Matching of players.

- Equipment and facility needs—Basketball can be played with a minimum of essential equipment, but players need to have the following personal items:

    ✓ Shoes and socks (Shoes should be designed specifically for court games like basketball, in which stopping, starting, and side-to-side movements are necessary.)

    ✓ Shorts

    ✓ T-shirt or jersey top (preferably numbered and with reversible colors if possible)

    ✓ Ball—All players should be encouraged (but not required) to purchase their own ball of the appropriate size and quality to use to improve their skills after practice and to make more balls available during practice. (See size recommendations in Chapter 2 of *Basketball Skill Progressions*.) You should attempt to obtain the optimum "one ball per every two players" for practice.

The most challenging equipment/facility issue is finding the appropriate basketball court and baskets for specific age-level competition. If at all possible, baskets should be height-adjustable from seven feet to 10 feet. Floor tape can be used to modify the free throw lane and line distance, while crosscourt or half-court modifications can be made to adjust court size.

Player safety should always be of paramount concern. The basketball experience for young people should be emotionally and physically safe for every child. The "fun and fundamentals" philosophy ensures emotional safety, but coaches also need to be accountable for physical safety. This can be accomplished through:

- Daily inspection of equipment and facilities
- Injury prevention and emergency plans
- Warnings of inherent risks in basketball
- Sequential, progressive skill development (see *Basketball Skill Progressions*)
- General supervision at all times (i.e., you must be present) and more specific supervision when teaching/practicing the more risky contact skills (e.g., taking a charge, defending a lay-up, rebounding, defending). These situations call for a higher level of injury prevention, care, and attention. The facility and court should be checked for hazards before each practice and competition (e.g., extra balls on the floor, dust, dirt, or fluid on the floor surface, unpadded vertical wall surfaces near the floor).

Practice Plans

Because a season plan may only include between 10 and 30 practice sessions, it is important to utilize all available practice time. A basic practice-plan format should be followed, but with some flexibility for adjustments along the way. (Also see *Basketball Skill Progressions* and the *Practicing to Play the Game* video.)

Collaborate and create a plan

Basic Practice Outline Sample

- Meet and greet/preview (5 to 10 minutes)—theme of the day, rule of the day, and equipment needed
- Warm-up (5 minutes)—should include basic skills
- Fundamentals and fast break (15 minutes)—the basic skills and some full-court work (you can use the games and/or the skills and drills approach)
- Team tactics and strategy (30 to 60 minutes)—offense, defense, transition game, and special situations
- Cool-down/meet and homework/review (5 to 15 minutes)—practice summary, assign skills for homework

Detailed Practice Schedule Sample

Practice #3—Monday, November 7
- Theme—quick stance with the ball
- Character/values—earn respect
- Rule of the day—traveling (starts and stops)
- Focus—passing and catching

6:50–7:00: Prepractice help—John, Sara, and Leon

7:00–7:05: Meet/preview—whistle for attention and review the theme, value, rule, and focus for the day

7:05–7:15: Warm-up—two-line passing lay-ups (make 10 in a row, left and right)

7:15–7:30: Fundamentals
- Skills: Passing and catching
- Critical Cues
  ✓ Pass with the feet on the floor and catch with the feet in the air
  ✓ Pass with a ping and catch with a click
  ✓ Pass to a hand target and catch with the eyes
- Games/drills
  ✓ Three-on-three half-court game (three passes before a shot)
  ✓ Discovery of deficient skills
  ✓ Three-on-three or three-on-two half-court game

7:30–8:00: Team offense and defense
- Three-on-three game, half-court to full-court (on defensive stop)—one transition
- One-on-one game, full-court—pressure the ball/guard the dribbler
- Critical Cues
  ✓ Quick stance (D)
  ✓ Ball-you-basket position
  ✓ Discovery
  ✓ One-on-one O-D zigzag drill
  ✓ One-on-one full-court again
- Four-on-four half-court to full-court

8:00–8:05: Cool-down
- Free-throw shooting (make 10)
- Critical Cues
  - ✓ Find dot
  - ✓ Bottom-of-shot bounce
  - ✓ Positive motion
  - ✓ Full follow-through (until net)
- Record the number of shots taken

8:05–8:10: Meet and review
- Come together/leader stretching
- Praise for theme/value/rule/focus
- Homework
  - ✓ 20 wall pass-and-catches
  - ✓ Make 20 free throws (record the number of shots taken)

Postpractice notes/evaluation
- More ballhandling practice needed
- Re-teach free throws next time
- Extra help—Mark, Bill, and Tommy
- Equipment needed: 6 balls
- Check the fit of shoes and make sure socks are put on properly with no wrinkles that could create blisters

Preplanning, even though difficult to accomplish, is necessary and will yield significant results. Checklists are provided in Appendix A to help you with the planning process.

5

Organization

"Providing direction and specific plans through organization promotes success, efficiency, and motion."

—Jerry Krause, Hall of Fame Coach

Overall planning for the season should be followed by more specific organization for practices and games. It is also necessary to organize such essential coaching tasks as selecting the squad, providing program essentials, and structuring a feeder program (i.e., a sequential, progressive youth basketball program for all ages).

Preseason Skills/Strategies Checklist

Regardless of the age level of your athletes, you need to establish a checklist that covers the skill and strategy details you must develop to properly prepare your team. This checklist can be added to your planning calendar for the season.

Team Offense

- Player-to-player offense
- Zone offense
- Press offense
- Defense-to-offense transition

- ✓ Primary (outnumbered) fast break
- ✓ Secondary (even-numbered) fast break
- Special situations
  - ✓ Jump ball
  - ✓ Out-of-bounds plays (sideline, end line)
  - ✓ Time and score
  - ✓ Free throws

Individual Offensive Progressions

- Footwork
  - ✓ Stance
  - ✓ Starts
  - ✓ Steps
  - ✓ Jumps
  - ✓ Stops
  - ✓ Moves without the ball
- Ballhandling
  - ✓ Passing and catching
  - ✓ vDribbling
  - ✓ Live-ball moves (post, perimeter)
- Shooting
  - ✓ Field goals (lay-ups, two-point field goals, and three-point field goals)
  - ✓ Free throws
- Offensive rebounding
- Setting and using screens
- Passing and cutting (give and go)

Team Defense

- Terms, numbering/naming (use one-syllable words—chair, shot, help, through, pick, stay, ball, post, front)
- Offense-to-defense transition
- Player-to-player (man) defense
- Zone defense (after eighth grade)
- Combination defense
- Match-up defense (advanced only)

Individual Defensive Progressions

- Footwork
  - ✓ Stance
  - ✓ Steps (step and slide, sprint)
- "On-ball" defense (ball-you-basket position)
  - ✓ Live ball (have not used dribble)
  - ✓ Guarding the dribbler
  - ✓ Dead ball (have used dribble)
  - ✓ Shooter
- "Off-ball" defense (ball-you-player-being-guarded position)
  - ✓ Closed (denial) stance—close to the ball
  - ✓ Open (pistols) stance—further from the ball
  - ✓ Post defense
- Special situations
  - ✓ Rebounding (blocking out)
  - ✓ Taking the charge
  - ✓ Helping and recover/rotating
  - ✓ Defending screens
  - ✓ Defending cuts

Miscellaneous

- Game preparation
  - ✓ Pregame
  - ✓ Time-outs
  - ✓ Halftime
  - ✓ Post-game
  - ✓ Bench organization
  - ✓ Substitutions
- Program assistants
  - ✓ Coach
  - ✓ Statisticians
  - ✓ Managers
  - ✓ Transportation

- Parents' roles
- Officials
- Equipment
- Facilities

Squad Selection

As coaches anticipate the beginning of the season, most of them can visualize the games and practices, as well as the skills they are going to be teaching. But in most coaching situations, before you can get to the teaching/playing phase, you must go through possibly the most difficult period of the season—squad selection. The more carefully you and your coaching staff can prepare for this phase of the season, the better it will be for both players and coaches.

Select by skill and ability

You must decide what physical skills you are looking for and how they will be tested and evaluated. Since physical skills are only part of the equation for being a successful athlete, you must determine the "attitude" skills you are looking for and how you can teach, measure, and evaluate those characteristics as well. Athletes should possess a combination of competence and character, and both aspects should be measured during squad selection. Expectations for the attitude of your team need to be established before the season begins and used during the selection process.

If you can keep every athlete who desires to play, you are fortunate. One of the goals of youth sports should be to be as inclusive as possible, but a selection process is eventually part of most programs. Squad selection is never easy. The clearer you can be to your potential players regarding your expectations for the effort, behavior, roles, and skills that you looking for, the easier it will be for everyone involved. You need to devise a fair and unbiased method to select players for the team. After you have identified potential players and have them all on the court, it is essential that you have planned practice according to the number of players turning out, the amount of court space, the number of baskets, and the number of coaches and teaching stations you have available.

It is important for you to balance the desire to give each player sufficient opportunities to show his ability and skills with the feeling of urgency you have to get the selection process completed and move on to regular practice. Not all of the selection process can be objective; part of selecting every team will come down to the subjective judgment by you, the coach. Drills and teaching stations must reflect both objective measures and subjective-judgment opportunities for the coaching staff.

Squad selection will proceed more efficiently if you do the following:
- Tell the players ahead of time which drills and tests will be used during the tryout, which gives each player the same opportunity to prepare.
- Select some drills that will demonstrate the players' ability to learn quickly. Explain to them the importance of establishing who is a quick learner. Then teach the skill and drill being used.
- Have each station (if practice plans include station drills) involve the same amount of time (e.g., 35 to 40 seconds), so that rotation from station to station is efficient.
- Give players (whenever possible) more than one attempt on tests and record either the average or the best score they achieve.
- Provide each coach or person testing with a roster and exact instructions for administering the test that they are conducting. Observe the test to ensure that the test is being conducted as you intended.

How to Announce the Final Roster

It requires a lot of courage to try out for a team and risk potential public failure, especially if a player is not one of the better athletes. Those players who are "on the bubble" may be too nervous to perform at their best. It is essential that every coach and player dignify the efforts of every player. Coaches need to go to extremes to make sure that players feel that they had a fair opportunity, and to make them feel valued regardless of their abilities and skills. If a player has enough courage to try out for a team, you must have enough courage to deal face-to-face with those players you are not choosing for the team. Posting lists excuses the coach from the responsibility he has to talk to and encourage the players who do not make that year's team to continue playing. It also provides peers who did not have the courage to turn out with an opportunity to ridicule those who did not make it.

Calling and talking to each player on the phone is preferable to any impersonal method, but the best method is to talk to the players throughout the entire process. You should ask players how they think they are doing and find out if they have been given a chance to showcase their best skills. If a player says that he has not had a chance to show what he is capable of, ask what you can do to make that happen. Often, it may be as simple as being paired with better players. Once a player has said that the coaches have seen him at his best, then it is okay to tell him where he stands. Players can be told during practice if they are in danger of not making the team and should have the opportunity to meet with you immediately afterward. Breaking the news gradually and in person gives the player more time to digest the news, as well as an opportunity to discuss his situation with you one-on-one. You should not feel like all roster choices need to be made on the same day. Times may arise when it is better to give some players another day or two to practice with a couple of extra players. Work hard to deliver your decisions as gracefully as possible and try to end each such conversation with a handshake and a "thank you," as well as with suggestions about where else a player might be able to play (other teams or leagues).

Full Participation

One of the things that will make squad selection better for players, coaches, and parents is to have another place where each child can play. Ideally, your community will have multiple layers of ability-based teams, so that players who may not have made one team can find a level where they can play and successfully compete. It is not a bad idea to have a method whereby players can move up a level during the season if they have been incorrectly assessed in tryouts or if they make enough improvement during the season.

You cannot possibly correctly identify from a group of players ages eight to 10 who will be the most proficient at ages 16 to 18. Experts in motor learning clearly state that skill level during middle school and junior high school is a poor predictor of later skill potential (in high school and college). Encourage all players to stay with the game as long as possible by providing playing opportunities for them in your community.

The goal for a youth program should be to get as many young people playing and learning to love the sport as possible. Don't run kids off or keep them from the game. The purpose of having multiple levels of play is that each athlete can participate at a level where he can experience some challenges and some successes.

Limit waiting time

Subjective evaluation of talent to place players on ability-level-based teams is difficult and mistakes will always happen—especially if player selection is done in a limited amount of time. Young athletes make physical changes rapidly and at different ages. Each year is a new and different year (same names, different players). Each player is capable of being passed by or moving past others, based on some things out of their control (physical maturity) and some things within their control (work habits).

In this age of athletic specialization, a dramatic change has taken place in the experience provided to our youth. Fewer and fewer students are trying out for organized sports, which are being left to only the athletically gifted, "year-round specialist" who is attempting to compete. Across America, close to 75 percent of all young people are finished with organized sports at age 15. Research says that there are six reasons young athletes lose their natural love and motivation for games:

• Fun is gone (number one reason)
• Consistent defeats
• Negative coaching
• Mental and physical fatigue
• Outside pressure (e.g., from parents)
• Too much complexity in the game

Another factor that has reduced the number of people who are playing is that institutions (schools in particular) have eliminated the opportunities for all but the most

Everyone plays

physically gifted. How many young people are losing the chance to learn all the great lessons that come from being coached, being part of a functional team, being part of something bigger than themselves, and learning from both winning and losing? Yes, full participation presents the obvious problems of adequate gym space, practice and game-time, qualified coaches, and money, but the problems caused by "elite-only" participation or lack of a middle-level athletic program are much more costly in the long run. The creation of such teams may mean having to practice in the mornings or later in the evenings to acquire enough gym space to allow all athletes to be active and involved.

Do you remember what it was like to be "cut" from the squad—to not see your name on the list? You enjoyed the game, and you just wanted to play and be with your friends, but the message was that you were not able to participate in sports or represent your school because you were not skilled or mature enough. What if schools used the same "elite-only" approach to other areas of education and only taught the top 15 math or history students? This practice would not be acceptable in anyone's eyes.

If you are a high school coach, do you realize how many potential athletes are being discouraged from your sport before they ever reach their full potential? If you are a youth or middle-level coach, how many mistakes are made in player evaluation because you had to select 15 players from the 100 turning out after just a couple of tryout days? How many times have you seen a "Little League all-star" who was physically mature at age 13 be passed up in high school by the athletes he used to dominate? What about the youngster who is not ready for pressure-filled competition but loves to play and just wants to learn? How about those players who give up forever after failing on their first attempt?

A youth or middle-level coach should not be a barrier builder. Instead he should eliminate as many of the obstacles and frustrations as possible to allow total participation, teach the fundamentals, and facilitate enjoyment of the game. Full participation, when done correctly, allows for each athlete to find a level of competition at which he can experience some success. Advanced players, who are ready for intense, daily practices, are able to have their needs met. Other athletes just learning the game can move to the levels that allow enjoyment, improvement, and success. Your responsibility to the youth at the middle levels does not stop with the top 15 athletes. By providing an athletic learning experience for everyone interested and committed, your school or community can meet many of the goals of the ideal youth sport program and middle-level education. Teach kids to love the game and build a broad base of athletes able to experience the values of sport. This system allows everyone to share in the joy of community or school pride, builds self-esteem by eliminating fear of failure, establishes a positive learning environment with clear expectations, and provides opportunities that take into account the tremendous physical and emotional differences among early adolescents. Don't think of this as watering down the program, but rather as building up quality at every skill level.

The definition of full participation should include clearly stated school-district or community goals concerning the special needs of middle-level students. Every athlete who meets the requirement to participate should have the opportunity to receive all the benefits of the sport they choose. Team activities that lend themselves to smaller numbers of competitors (e.g., volleyball, basketball, baseball, softball) should provide teams of 12 to 15 people with required playing-time rules. Provide as many teams, coaches, and schedules as necessary to satisfy the number of participants (e.g., 120 athletes turning out for basketball would result in a varsity squad of 15 players and seven to 10 additional teams of 10 to 15 players, with the teams named using colors or college nicknames according to the sport. Athletes should be placed on teams based on relative ability so that they may compete on an equal basis with teams from other schools. Cooperation is required to allow athletes the flexibility to move within the framework of the program to find the level where they can most successfully compete as they improve.

Activities that can be conducted in larger groups (e.g., wrestling, track, football) or on an individual basis (e.g., tennis, badminton) can be organized into ladders according to age and skill levels. The coaches only need to identify methods to allow each participant to compete on an equal basis.

True full-participation programs certainly present problems, but school districts and communities only need to examine the needs of early adolescents to justify the money it requires to allow every individual the opportunity to enjoy the benefits of athletic participation.

Basketball Essentials

Essentials of a Good Team

- Play hard every day
- Win the individual battles on defense
- Win the rebound battle on both ends of the floor
- Get good shots and get more of them
- React with fundamentals in the "unplanned" part of the game
- Know and embrace your role and understand your strengths and limitations
- Don't worry about mistakes made with full effort and focus. Get on with the next play. (Think *WIN—what's important now?*)

Essentials for Good Defense

- Remember: talk, technique, position, and effort
- Create an "unplanned play"
- Keep the ball out of the middle
- Do not allow easy or uncontested shots
- Do not allow second shots

Essentials for a Good Fast Break

- Get a defensive stop/defensive block-out
- Outlet to a decision-maker
- Take off
- Make good decisions on the move
- Maintain an attack mentality
- Attain an offensive rebounding position
- Achieve defensive balance—safety position

Essentials for a Good Half-Court Offense

- Have balance—spacing and timing
- Understand the optimum number of passes for your level

- Know and fulfill your role
- Have good timing on cuts and screens
- Make solid contact on legal screens
- Use purposeful movement
- Make the "easy play"
- Get a good first shot
- Get a better second shot—offensive rebounding position
- Achieve defensive balance—safety position

The Six Most Unselfish Plays in Basketball

- Helping a teammate who got beat
- Taking a charge
- Passing to someone with a better shot
- Setting a screen that gets a teammate a shot
- Committing to an offensive rebound—not needing to take the first shot
- Embracing all roles as equal in value—12-on-five basketball

Helping Players Reach the Next Level in a Feeder Program

In most communities, the highest level of play most young athletes can achieve is the local high school program. Although the primary role of youth sports is to have the athletes enjoy the experience and learn life lessons regardless of ability, some athletes have the ability and the desire required to have a realistic goal of playing for the high school. If you are in a community where you can predict what high school your athletes will attend, then you are part of the "feeder program." Since only a few athletes are still playing basketball by their senior year, the sole purpose of youth programs should not be to prepare players for that opportunity. But you should know which players have a goal of playing at the next level and be ready to help them improve their skills and attitudes to give them the best chance to succeed.

Many factors must be considered when you are trying to pass a player on to the next coach and the next level, but the following guidelines make the transition of these players easier and more effective. When transitioning players, you need to take your own ego out of the equation and do whatever is going to allow your players the best chance to play for the next coach.

Communication

Possibly the most essential ingredient to successfully transition players through the system is to devise a clear and consistent communication plan between the high school coach and all the feeder coaches. Communication and player assessment are key parts of each coach's responsibility. Take the time to meet and get to know all the people who are working with local players.

Offenses and Defenses

Two theories exist about which offense and defense the feeder coaches should run. The first theory supports running the exact same style as the high school. The second theory allows each coach to run his own offenses and defenses based upon his personal knowledge or the abilities of his players. You should ask the high school coach which theory they want you to adhere to, and then do whatever they prefer. If the high school coach chooses to have you run their offenses and defenses, then they need to be willing to spend the time necessary to teach the feeder coaches how they can successfully break it down to the skill level of the younger players.

Terminology and Technique

Many ways exist to teach and name the same skills, just as different ideas exist on how to correctly execute those skills. More important than the running of the exact offense and defense of the local high school is the consistent use of terminology—words you use to initiate action and communicate and teach technique. Basketball comes with its own language and often the same skill can have several different descriptive "trigger" words or critical cues. It would be wise for all coaches in your program to use the exact same terms, as this system will allow the players to use the same language each season.

For example, consider the act of defending a backdoor cut. One coach may want his players to "drop-step and open to the ball," while another coach may insist that each player "swivel his head and put out a stop sign with his baseline hand." Both techniques work, but it would be better for the athlete if the feeder coach found out what technique and terms the high school coach uses and then taught it that way. Again, whatever you have to do to give your kids the best chance to understand and perform the skill is all that is important. Share all terminology and teach it like it was your own.

Fundamental Skills

All excellent feeder programs have a sound fundamental skill (technique) base that is taught sequentially and progressively at all age levels. From the time a young athlete enters a youth basketball program, he should be exposed to the same fundamentals and terminology as he progresses through the feeder program. A carefully developed fundamental skill approach, with terms and appropriate age/skill/equipment modifications, is presented in *Basketball Skill Progressions*.

Ask for Help When You Need It

Coaches who put kids first should never hesitate to ask for help. You need to know where you can get information and knowledge to make you as effective as possible. Information can come from conversations, observation, books, and videos. Most coaches who have been in the profession for any length of time have built a coaching network (i.e., people who they can call for advice) and a coaching library.

Youth coaches may want to seek counsel or help in the following areas:
- Terminology and technique—Go through your terms and techniques and then break down drills used to teach each of those techniques.
- Shared expertise on the fundamentals of the game—Developing players who are fundamentally sound makes everyone's job easier.
- Time management—Develop a checklist of essentials for your age group. Keep in mind that most youth coaches have much less practice time than higher-level coaches. High school coaches may have 50 to 60 two-hour practices during the season (totaling as much as 120 hours), while a youth coach may only have 10 to 15 practices of one and a half hours each (totaling as few as 15 hours).
- Practice planning—Effectively use the time you have to get the most accomplished. Consider time spent teaching individual vs. team concepts, drills vs. scrimmage, part vs. whole, etc.
- How to teach a physical skill—Coaches who have been trained as physical educators understand the rules of motor learning. To effectively teach a physical skill, follow the progression of defining, modeling, shaping, and reinforcing.
- How to balance discipline and fun—Observe coaches who have been able to establish a team climate of focused attention and who can make the work seem enjoyable.
- How to work with parents—Relationships with parents often determine the longevity of a coach's tenure. Experienced and successful coaches have learned how to communicate with parents so that they understand their role and, therefore, make the experience better for everyone involved.
- How to deal with officials—It is easy for inexperienced coaches to lose focus of the parts of the game over which they have control.

Keeping Kids in the Program

One of the keys to successful high school programs is to have a wide base of players from which to draw. Don't run kids off. Youth coaches should try to develop an interest and love of the game in as many kids as possible. Until kids are about 10 or 11, your first responsibility is to teach them to love the game, so that they leave practice and want to go home and shoot some more with their mom or dad. At about age 12 or 13, the focus can be equally divided between loving the game and learning the game. Remember, one of the things that ruins the natural love for the game is "making it too complex." Keep basketball simple and easy to learn.

Attributing Success to Preparation

Hopefully your team will have some success (even if you have to create those successes in practice). When younger players experience success, it will be helpful to them and to the next coach to have them learn to attribute their success to preparation. Focusing on preparation makes practices more meaningful. Both wins and losses can be traced to preparation. Losses can always teach players that they are capable of, and responsible for, getting better. Teach them that "confidence is based on proper preparation."

Setting the "Attitude" Tone—Clear Behavioral Standards

Feeder coaches can help a high school coach by setting and holding to behavioral standards. The players for whom it is most important to be held accountable for appropriate athletic behavior are often the most highly skilled. Establish behavioral standards and demand correct team behavior during all games and practices.

The most important gift you can give your players and to the high school coach is to teach your players to have a positive athletic attitude. Players who can focus for two hours, take correction as a compliment, practice hard, and always put the team ahead of themselves are the most likely to succeed at the next level.

Mastery of Individual Skills Within a Team Concept

Individual skills are essential, but always within the team concept. Coaches who teach "get yours" at the expense of the team are doing kids and the high school coach a disservice. The team should always come first.

Support and Loyalty

Feeder coaches must speak supportively to parents and players about the high school coach, program, team, and the school itself. Your first responsibility is to work to build an allegiance. Even if your personal relationship with the high school coach is not good, being critical will not help the athletes.

Helping Parents Understand Their Role

Take the time to teach parents how to really help performance during competition (see Chapter 7).

The Narrowing Pyramid

Athletes and parents need to understand how the pyramid narrows as the children get older. Fewer and fewer kids get the opportunity to continue playing at a competitive level as they enter high school. Most people who play youth basketball will not make their junior high team. Most players who make their junior high team will not make the high school junior varsity. And most players who make the junior varsity team will probably not make the high school varsity. In many communities, 100 youngsters may be participating at the fifth-grade level, but only four to eight are still playing on the team by the time they are seniors in high school. Allow the athletes to enjoy the experience while they are still playing and prepare them for a time when they may not play as much, or at all. Children must not to hang their self image on playing well—or playing at all. Teach them that their value as a person is not dependent on athletic success. It is best not to focus on a goal of earning college scholarships, as they will not be available to more than 99.9 percent of young players.

Early-Maturing Athletes

A player who has matured early may be the best player for the feeder coach. All coaches have seen the fully matured, six-foot-tall sixth grader who turns out to be a six-foot-tall senior. It is critical that you recognize and counsel the parents of "early maturers," along with the athlete, so they all understand that he will not always be the biggest, fastest, or strongest, and may have to be realistic about his athletic future as others catch up and/or surpass him. Many early-maturing athletes can continue to be successful if they are willing to alter their role or position and continue to work when success doesn't come so easily.

Late-Maturing Athletes

Feeder coaches have an equal responsibility to counsel "late maturers" and "overachievers," so that they do not get discouraged because they are not having much success early on. Remind them that their best days may be coming, that they must not give up, and that the game that is so difficult right now will get easier and easier. You never know who is going to grow six inches or wear out a basketball over the summer. One of the best scenarios is the 5'4" seventh grader who grows up learning guard skills and grows into a 6'4" senior who can handle the ball and shoot from the perimeter.

Establish and Maintain a Physical Connection

Go out of your way to provide opportunities for your players to be around the high school coach and team. Provide a schedule of games and practices and a time for the high school coach to meet and speak to your team. Create times for the older players to be around the younger ones (camps, big brother/little brother programs). Younger players need mentors and model older players, and older players can benefit when they learn to teach younger players (the ultimate test of their own learning). Both groups can learn the life lesson of serving others and giving back to the game by spending time together. It is helpful to both parties any time older players can spend time coaching the younger ones.

Feeder coaches should be seen as part of the "whole program" and the "whole staff." Let the high school coach know that you would like to be included as part of the bigger picture. A wise high school coach will use people willing to volunteer in any way that they would like to be involved (scouting, game planning, attending clinics). The end-of-the-year banquet should always include all the coaches who have ever worked with the seniors.

One of the great things about coaching kids at an earlier age is that you get to be in their lives for a long time. Look for opportunities to keep in contact with your athletes (e.g., summer leagues, camps, post-game meetings, practices). High school coaches should always open up their locker rooms to those people who have given time and energy in their athletes' lives.

6

Game Coaching

"Proper planning and practice preparation result in players and teams who face few surprises. They are prepared to play the game."

—Jerry Krause, Hall of Fame Coach

It has been said that most real coaching takes place in practice, when players learn the basic skills and team strategies. However, young players need to experience game competition to meet the challenges encountered in that setting. Due to young athletes' inexperience, games offer significant challenges—physically, skill-wise, and emotionally. They offer excitement as well as apprehension for beginning players.

Even though coaches carry out most game preparation in practices and before games occur, ample opportunities still exist for learning on game day, especially during the "teachable moments" that often happen before, during, and after games. These emotionally charged periods are golden opportunities to impact young players, hopefully in a positive way. It is very important that you recognize that games can have a real impact on youngsters. The goal is to make that impact as positive as possible.

You and your players should approach challenging games with an even keel. Young people closely observe the conduct of coaches during games and tend to emulate their approach. You are strongly encouraged to become aware of your game conduct and coaching style during games. Approach each game as a testing/learning

Time-out—a teachable moment

opportunity for all players and coaches. As much as possible, allow all of your players an equal chance to participate. Games should be viewed as part of a process that allows players and teams to test their skills and meet the challenge of competition. Focus on performance, not just the game's outcome. In the words of John Wooden, teach players to "win with humility and lose with dignity" as they strive to become their best, regardless of ability.

Game Checklist

Pregame

- Dressing—shoes, socks, shorts, and uniform top
- Mental/emotional preparation—teach your players what to expect and how to prepare for games (the good, the bad, and the ugly)
- Warm-ups—five to 15 minutes of fundamental skills, including shooting. Rehearse, develop, and teach proper warm-up technique to get players used to gradually warming up to game speed.
- Team meeting—usually takes place before the warm-ups to give final reminders and assure players of success and remind them to focus on fun
- Team huddling—focus on a "team" or "value" theme, as embodied in a word or phrase as they break the huddle (e.g., respect, team, defense)

Game Preparation

- Jump balls
  - ✓ Lineup
  - ✓ Positions
  - ✓ Responsibilities
- Team offense(s)
  - ✓ Player-to-player
  - ✓ Zone
  - ✓ Transition (defense to offense)—fast break
  - ✓ Out-of-bounds plays (side, under)
  - ✓ Free throws
- Team Defense(s)
  - ✓ Player-to-player
  - ✓ Zone
  - ✓ Transition (offense to defense)—rules, strategy
  - ✓ Out-of-bounds plays
  - ✓ Free throws

Miscellaneous

- Time-outs
  - ✓ Calling
  - ✓ Content (get their attention, impart one or two concepts, give more information than emotion)
- Halftime
  - ✓ Recovery
  - ✓ Brief message
  - ✓ Warm-ups
- Post-game
  - ✓ Cool-down
  - ✓ Meeting (review one or two game concepts)
  - ✓ Assignment/lessons learned—give them time and space to recover and focus on the next practice

Teaching strategies

A Good Game

To get the best experience from a good game, you must have several key ingredients. The best game experiences result from good players, good coaching, and good officials. The common theme that should be stressed is respect—developing self-respect to build self-confidence and earn the respect of others. Respect is essential between players and coaches, players and officials, and especially coaches and officials. The guiding principles should be the golden rule—"treat others as you would like to be treated"—and the silver rule—"don't treat others as you wouldn't want to be treated." Ensure that you and your players know the rules, but never question a judgment call by the officials. Set up a system or plan that allows all players an equal chance to practice and play at all levels of youth basketball.

Game Coaching Tips and Thoughts

The Coach's Role

- Decide what kind of a leadership style you want to have as a coach during the game. Your job is to create the proper environment so that athletes play to their potential and behave in a manner that represents your philosophy, the school, and the team.
- Coach for the love of the game and the respect of the athlete.
- Always put athletes' needs above winning.

- Accept and abide by the judgment of the officials, and think of the rules of the game as "mutual agreements" required to play within the spirit of the game.
- Lead with character and by example.
- Constantly work to improve your knowledge and ability to teach the game and the athletes.
- Be willing to confront incorrect behavior or less than all-out effort.
- Keep the game simple, easy to learn, and fun.
- Develop a "positive-demanding" coaching style.

Game Coaching—Style Check

- Decide what coaching style you want to have and work toward controlling yourself during the emotional parts of the game. You must be able to model that style. Who do you want to be during the game?
- Controlling your emotions
  - ✓ Learn to manage your moods—to stay calm in pressure situations—keeping in mind that the game of basketball is being played by innocent, immature children (youth sports), inconsistent, highly emotional teenagers (high school and college), or egotistical, me-first adults (pros).
  - ✓ If you are unable to control your emotions, you will find yourself saying and doing things that you wish you had not. You cannot let your emotions control your brain—your brain is your most important weapon during any game.
- Style Check
  - ✓ Aggressive, passive, or somewhere in between
  - ✓ Be involved in every decision
  - ✓ Be involved in every referee's call
  - ✓ For what kind of coach would you like to play?
  - ✓ Where is your attention focused—on things you have control over or things you can't control but are trying to control? What can you control during the game?
  - ✓ Do you think that you can influence the referees? Is it worth it?
  - ✓ Keep the athletes as the main focus. Some coaches feel the need to be the center of attention (active, yelling), but this makes the athletes learn to wait for other people to do their thinking for them.
- Identify and use only behaviors that will help team performance during competition. What coaching behaviors help performance? What behaviors hinder performance?
- General principles to incorporate into your style and questions to ask yourself
  - ✓ Modeling confidence, concentration, and poise is the single most important contribution that you can make to your athletes.

✓ Show your players the face they need to see, remembering that your composure will become theirs. Your body language may say more than your words and players need positivity when things are not going well. They need you to be calm when the pressure is on. Put yourself in your athletes' shoes during a pressure situation. If you do not want players to panic or play nervously, then you cannot display those characteristics.

✓ How would your players describe you and your emotions in pressure situations?

✓ How do you want your athletes to respond to adversity? Respond to adversity the way you want your athletes to respond. They will do what you do.

✓ Treat officials as you expect your players to treat them (with respect).

✓ Be consistent. Be the same person you are in practice and focus on the performance of your team, not on opponents, refs, or other game conditions. Use the same language, reinforcement, motivation, techniques, and tone of voice as you do in practice.

✓ Find a style that will allow players to maintain their confidence, composure, and concentration, regardless of the situation. If they are feeling uncertain, you must show them confidence. If they are feeling hopeless, you must give them hope. If they are feeling overconfident, then you must let them know they are in for a battle.

✓ Remember to use positive reinforcement. If you are a positive coach in practice, you need to be a positive coach in competition.

✓ Work hard. Make each game a chess match or a puzzle. Are you a thinker or a reactor?

✓ Do not excuse yourself by saying, "I've taught you that" (reteach it and teach it better) or "you panic in the clutch" (always keep your poise)

• After the game
  ✓ Take responsibility for all losses and give players credit for all wins.

  ✓ Control your emotions and think ahead. Plan what you are going to do when you feel like you might not keep your composure. If necessary, talk with an assistant before you speak to the team.

  ✓ Give yourself and the players a chance to cool off, step back, and get a bigger perspective.

  ✓ If you can't end on a positive note, say nothing at all and wait until the next day.

• To be the kind of game coach you want to be:
  ✓ Have someone come and watch and evaluate your coaching

  ✓ Videotape yourself

  ✓ Make an audiotape of yourself

  ✓ Ask your athletes how they see you as a coach

- Final questions for game coaches:
  - ✓ Does your game behavior represent your philosophy?
  - ✓ Does your game behavior exemplify the behavior you want from fans and players?
  - ✓ Do you display any behavior that would entice new fans?
  - ✓ Does your game behavior demonstrate the type of respect you expect from your athletes toward the officials, opponents, and opposing coaches?
  - ✓ How do you respond when your athletes do not meet behavioral expectations during the game?
  - ✓ Do you respect the judgment of the contest officials, who are abiding by the rules of the event?

Game-Day Motivation

Before the Game

Athletes need to learn how to get themselves ready for competition. The longer you coach, the more you will realize just how different each of your athletes is and that everyone prepares differently. Athletes use many different "readying" methods to prepare to perform their best, and each person must discover what methods work best for him. You cannot assume that your athletes will all follow the same "readying" procedure or that they will prepare the same way from year to year.

If an athlete isn't motivated to play, he needs to look at himself rather than some outside source. He also needs to understand the difference between being "psyched up" and being motivated. Too much excitement may have a negative impact on performance, especially in sports like basketball that require fine motor skills. Your job is to provide as many methods as possible to ensure that each player can discover the best method for him and is prepared at game time. One of the key things you need to understand is how to determine how much motivation is required and make sure that the team is in the correct frame of mind to begin a game. Every team is going to be different. With some, you may have to model a sense of urgency and be high-spirited, and with others you may need to demonstrate reduced levels of energy.

Athletes should also focus on their preparation, individual and team assignments, and keys to meet performance goals. Remind them of times when they have performed well, whether it was in a practice or a game.

During the Game

No coach can ever predict exactly how a game will go. For coaches, games are simply puzzles waiting to be solved. Each game will bring a different set of circumstances and require you to see the big picture. One of your goals for game day should be to eliminate surprises for players. In other words, players should simply be doing what has been practiced, and doing it as hard as possible.

"No surprises" also applies to you. Be the same person in a game that you are during practice. If you are low-key and soft-spoken during practice and then a wild screamer with a dramatic sense of urgency during games, you will confuse your players.

As the game gets underway, focus on the things you can control and don't waste your energy on anything out of your control. Remember to respond to effort and behavior, not just performance or outcome. You are trying to establish a tie between a desired behavior and your reinforcement.

Provide and model positive energy and direction for your team. Verbally pat your team on the back and look for the good in every situation. Try to not substitute directly after mistakes, only to give corrections that are probably already evident to the athlete. When you want to provide corrective feedback, choose times when the athlete is going to be receptive. During the game is not the time to do a lot of talking. Keep your instructions quick and simple and do not waste any words. Too many coaches talk just to be talking. When you use your voice, it should get immediate attention and relay an exact message to the player(s). Use the same verbal cues that were used in practice, so each player can quickly assimilate your meaning and carry it over into his actions. Think about what you are going to say before you say it, and if you have any doubts, keep it to yourself. In most game situations, the players are already overloaded and don't need much additional stimuli or information. Also, be extremely aware of the messages your body language is sending. Be careful of the way it can be interpreted by players, spectators, and officials. Facial expressions can carry tremendous power.

Try not to overreact to mistakes. Instead, make mental or physical notes for the next practice, when the opportunity to learn is improved. Whenever possible, allow your players to compete through mistakes and misfortune, which not only teaches them to quickly get over their mistakes and continue competing, but also demonstrates your confidence in them. Stay positive and aggressive if you expect your players to compete that way. Show your enjoyment of the games and your players' efforts with quick, simple expressions of appreciation.

Time-Outs

Use time-outs to get one or two ideas across, wait, and then watch your players' eyes for acknowledgment. Then, repeat your instructions. Be positive and direct, but don't try to give too much information too fast.

Allow your players to relax and get water for the first 10 to 15 seconds of a time-out, while you gather your thoughts (by yourself or with assistant coaches). Think about using a "buddy system" to have the players help motivate each other and keep their heads in the game. Every player in the game has a partner (or two) on the bench who greets him as he returns to the bench. That player tries to have one good thing to say to him and one suggestion to make during the first 10 to 15 seconds of the time-out. The "buddy" should also have the last word during the time-out. Try to have players match up by position so they are able to give technical help and also watch the game from the correct perspective. This technique also keeps the players on the bench involved and prepared to enter the game.

Halftime

Halftime provides a chance to rest, regroup, and prepare. It is a good idea to rehearse what you are going to do at halftime in practice before you play a game. To do this, simply take a "halftime" during one of your practices. For the first few minutes, allow players to take care of personal needs, while you meet with coaches and determine your main two or three focuses to begin the second half. Meet with any individual players who need specific instruction. Do not spend time talking to one player in front of the whole team. Finally, meet with the team and keep a fine focus. End with a "positive-aggressive" statement, keeping their focus on the goals you had for the game. Leave yourself enough time for the team to warm up physically. Remain with the players and prepare them to play hard during the first few minutes of the second half.

After the Game

Keep post-game meetings short and positive. Realize that everyone will have a reaction to how the game was played, and these reactions will be from their individual perspectives. Win or lose, first provide a few minutes for players to escape the surroundings of the game and cool down. The locker room needs to be a private and safe place for athletes and teams at all times.

You have an opportunity to set the focus after a game. Practice what you are going to do during the post-game period before it arrives, especially when you feel frustrated. Letting your anger come out directly after a game is seldom productive, and anger often just a selfish reaction for you that can be hurtful to young athletes. You may forget what you said in a few minutes, but your words may stay with an athlete for a lifetime.

Holding onto your frustrations after a game is a test of your mental toughness. Learn to control your emotions and model the mental toughness you expect from your team.

Your assessment will be much more effective and accurate when you have had time to think about it, and also to review the game tape. More often than not, corrections made immediately after the game are revealed as incorrect once you had time to watch video. Take time to think about your reactions and keep corrections to yourself until the next practice.

What most people need after competition is time and space (i.e., recovery time), so think about quick, positive endings. Regardless of the score of any game, your job is to stay optimistic and let that optimism show to your players. If you need to talk to individual players, do so after the team summary. *Win or lose, keep your athletes focused on performance, not on outcome.*

7

Team Roles and Sport: Know Your Role—Fill Your Role

"Call it a clan, a network, a tribe, or a family. Whatever you call it, whoever you are, you need one."

—Jane Howard, Writer

The involvement of parents in the athletic experience of children is a given. Without question, all parents should be part of this area of growth in their children's lives. Their involvement affects their own child, the coach, the rest of the team, the other parents, and the officials. Only parents can decide how they will be involved.

Most parents mean well, but they may not be aware of how they can meaningfully help the athletes reach their goals and improve performance. If handled correctly, with you and the team parents working together for the benefit of the athletes, the athletic experience can provide a tremendously positive developmental challenge for the participants. To ensure that the athletic experience is as positive as it should be, everyone involved (coaches and parents alike) must always remember that the needs of the children must come first.

Regardless of the age of the athletes or the sport being played, only five roles exist at any athletic contest:

- Player
- Coach
- Official
- Parent
- Game/league administrator

Everyone involved in athletics who chooses to attend a game would be wise to choose only one of these roles and fulfill it to the best of his ability. Each of these roles carries its own set of responsibilities, which are presented in the following sections. Distribute these lists to everyone involved in your athletic program and be available to answer any questions.

A Player's Role

- Play the game for fun.
- Be gracious when you win (humility) and graceful when you lose (dignity).
- Respect and abide by the rules of the game.
- Put the team ahead of yourself in every situation—be a great teammate.
- Accept decisions made by those in authority—coaches and officials.
- Demonstrate respect to, and earn respect from, your opponents, coaches, officials, and teammates.
- Be accountable for your own actions.
- Develop a teachable spirit that allows you to take correction as a compliment.
- Develop a "mistake mentality." Use mistakes as status reports on your improvement.
- Accept and embrace the discipline involved in athletics, because it benefits the team.
- Develop a feeling of pride based upon the "shared joy" of the team, and do not have pride that emanates from arrogance or a sense of entitlement.
- Be an athlete of character.

Players fill one role

A Coach's Role

- Coach for the love of the game and the love of the athlete—"child-centered coaching."
- Put the welfare of your athletes above winning.
- Develop a positive-demanding coaching style adjustable to the age of your players. Use encouragement and positive reinforcement as your primary methods of motivating players.
- Have a preseason meeting with parents to establish expectations for everyone involved.
- Keep the communication channels open throughout the season.
- Have realistic and clear expectations for all volunteers.
- Accept and abide by the judgment of the officials. View the rules of the league and the game as "mutual agreements" required to play within the spirit of the game.
- Look for and reward effort and behavior over outcome.
- Give dignity to mistakes made with at full speed and with full attention. Help players develop a "mistake mentality," meaning that they understand that mistakes are necessary for learning. Mistakes must be acknowledged, understood, and used as tools for correction and learning.
- Lead with character and by example, especially when things go poorly.
- Put the needs of the team ahead of those of any individual, but give every child attention during practice.
- Treat each person fairly, but not necessarily the same.
- Constantly work to improve your knowledge and ability to teach the game and the athletes.
- Be willing to confront incorrect behavior or less than all-out effort.
- Encourage multiple-sport participation.
- Keep the game simple, fun, and easy to learn.
- Be willing to work with parents for the benefit of the individual athlete.
- Be a confidence-builder.

An Official's Role

- Earn the respect of players, coaches, administrators, and other officials.
- Demonstrate respect for the game and the participants by maintaining integrity, neutrality, sensitivity, professionalism, discretion, and tactfulness within a "child-centered" philosophy.
- Assist as much as possible in teaching players basketball rules and the boundaries of the game.

- Possess and demonstrate a comprehensive knowledge of the rules of the game and the mechanics of officiating, so you can exercise your authority to enforce the rules impartially and effectively, as relevant to the level of play.
- Do your best to make the game safe and fair for all participants.
- Uphold the honor and dignity of the profession in all interactions with athletes, coaches, game administrators, and spectators.
- Demonstrate communication skills (both verbal and nonverbal) and actions that are above reproach.
- Work with the players, coaches, and spectators to promote an atmosphere of sportsmanship, courtesy, and self-control.
- Maintain clear, consistent control of the game.
- Do your part to teach the rules as boundaries of the game (both in spirit and intent). This teaching is your contribution to educational sports.
- Be involved in the league activities and build relationships with coaches and administrators.
- Arrive at the game prepared both mentally and physically and with sufficient time to inspect the facilities and equipment, give pregame instructions to timers and scorekeepers, and meet and consult with your partner and the coaches.
- Accept responsibility for all actions taken..

A Parent's Role

- Attend as many games as possible.
- Be a model, not a critic. Model appropriate behavior, poise, and confidence.
- Attend preseason team meetings, league orientations, and education programs.
- Do everything possible to make the athletic experience positive for your child and others. Put the goals of the children first.
- View the game with team goals in mind. Consistently support all the players, coaches, and officials.
- Attempt to relieve competitive pressure, not increase it.
- Encourage multiple-sport participation.
- Give the athletic experience to the athlete.
- Look upon opponents as friends involved in the same experience.
- Accept the judgment of the officials and coaches. Demonstrate respect and remain in control. Parents do not have the right to interact with a game official.
- Accept the results of each game and do not make excuses.
- Demonstrate winning with humility and losing with dignity.
- Focus on the athletic effort and improvement (e.g., athlete-owned "effort goals"), instead of the outcome.

- Dignify mistakes made by athletes who are giving their best effort (support development of a "mistake mentality").
- Allow the coach to be the one to offer advice and correction. Maintain an encouraging voice. Only the coach should have an instructional voice.
- Be an encourager. Encourage athletes to keep their perspective in both victory and defeat.
- Model correct behavior before, during, and after the games. What adults do in moderation, young people feel free to do in excess.
- Let the players play, the coaches coach, and the officials officiate without interference from the sideline.
- Be a good listener.
- Accept the goals, roles, and achievements of your child.
- After the game, give the athletes some time and space. Be a quiet, reflective listener and remind them why they are playing in the first place.
- Be a confidence-builder.

All adults involved in your program need to do their part to provide each athlete with the help and assistance he really needs to perform well. As such, remind your players' parents to address the following critical issues when discussing athletic participation with their children. Distribute this list to every parent prior to the season.

- Ask your child questions about why he plays and what his goals and roles are, and then accept his reasons as his own.

Parents—support only

- Once you know your child is safe physically and emotionally, release him to the experience (the game, the team, and the coach). All of your child's successes are his, as are all of the small problems and failures that come with the season.
- Allow the coach to be the one instructional voice.
- During the game, model poise and confidence and focus on the team.
- After the game, give your child space and time and leave him alone during his recovery time. Be a quiet, reflective listener if and when they choose to talk with you about their experience.
- Be a confidence-builder by maintaining a consistent perspective and not saying or doing anything that will make your child feel like his self-worth is somehow tied to playing time or the outcome of a game.

Remind each parent that if he is having difficulty dealing with officiating, he should remember that the officials are there to be in charge of the game, make subjective judgments, enforce the rules, and control play. When a parent criticizes a referee, he is teaching his children that it is okay to challenge authority. Some adults have the false impression that by being in a crowd, they become anonymous. People behaving poorly cannot hide. Remind parents that a seat at a youth basketball game is not a license to verbally abuse others or be obnoxious.

As the season begins, parents are encouraged to ask themselves the following questions. Again, it might be a good idea to distribute this list prior to the season.
- Do you want your child to play? If so, why?
- What will be a successful season for you as a parent?
- What are your goals for your child?
- What do you hope your child gains from the experience?
- What do you think your child's role will be on this team?

After a parent has honestly answered these questions, he should sit down with his child to discuss the upcoming season. Have each parent ask his child the following questions. When the child responds, the parent should just listen without talking.
- Why are you playing?
- What would make this a successful season for you?
- What goals do you have?
- What do you think your role will be on the team?

Once the parent has heard his child's answers, he must compare them to his own responses. It is ideal if the answers match. On the other hand, if the parent's responses are different from the child's, the parent must change his attitude and accept the goals and expectations of his child.

Parents should be fully aware of who is involved in their child's life. Once a parent feels comfortable and is not overly concerned for his child's physical and emotional safety, one of the best gifts he can give to his child is to release him to athletic activity as a learning experience (with failures and successes). As such, during the season, a parent must share his child with the coach and the team. The earlier a parent is able to do this, the better it is for the child's development and growth. If a parent feels the need to talk to a coach about a problem, he should call and allow the coach to choose an appropriate time and place to discuss the problem.

The following concerns are appropriate for a parent to discuss with his child's coach:
- Mental and physical treatment of the child
- Ways to help the child improve
- Concerns about the child's behavior

Inappropriate areas of concern that a parent should not discuss with his child's coaches include:
- Playing time
- Team strategy or play calling
- Other team members

When parents stop and analyze the value of athletic experience for their children, they often find that the primary reasons they want their kids to play sports is to benefit them physically, emotionally, and socially. Also, parents hope that something learned from the experience will allow their child to grow into a better adult, parent, and citizen. The side benefits of playing sports include that kids are given a good opportunity to learn how to work and get along with others, take good risks in a public arena and survive, learn to set and achieve goals by developing positive work habits, learn how to succeed and fail with dignity, and develop friendships outside the family unit that can last for a lifetime.

Relatively speaking, the athletic experience in school lasts a short time. Parents need to see the big picture, be a model, and bring their children back to reality when necessary. Every child is hoping that his parents will be part of their positive athletic memories.

Organization Leaders—League or Program Board of Directors

One part of the team may or may not be present during the game. The league or program directors have the ultimate responsibility for establishing overall philosophical standards for coaches, players, officials, and parents and following through with their enforcement and assessment. Therefore, they have a large role in the success of the experience.

League's Role

- Develop a written child-centered philosophy that will guide the actions of everyone involved—focusing on effort, improvement, skill mastery, positive reinforcement, sportsmanship, fun, and fundamentals (see Chapter 1).
- Communicate the program philosophy to every player, coach, official, and parent.
- Ensure the presence of qualified coaches and officials by:
  ✓ Doing background checks
  ✓ Providing basic first aid training and having emergency medical procedures in place and posted on the site
  ✓ Providing coaching and officiating education
- Have league standards—concerning game rules, playing time, number of games and practices, and standards of behavior by players, coaches, officials, and fans—very clearly written and understood.
- Develop age-appropriate playing rules, and monitor the number of practices and games.
- Attempt to achieve a competitive balance within the league.
- Have clear consequences for violations of your league standards that are consistently enforced.
- Recognize and reward positive behaviors of players, coaches, officials, and fans.
- Develop an environment of respect for officials, including zero tolerance for disputes regarding judgment calls.
- Evaluate the performance of coaches, officials, and parents in terms of meeting the behavioral standards of the league.
- Evaluate the program's effectiveness in terms of player enjoyment, skill improvement, and player retention.

Fill One, and Only One, Sports Role

As a final reminder, worthwhile sport experiences for young people depend upon clearly defined roles for all involved: players, coaches, officials, parents, and administrators. It is imperative that each group clearly understand and appreciate its unique role and carry it out as well as possible. Everyone should focus on his unique role in providing the best basketball experience for all young players.

8

Developing Essential Playing Skills

"Basketball is nothing more than developing and executing the basic skills for recreation and competition."

—Ralph Miller, Naismith Hall of Fame Coach

Because of the need to focus on fun and fundamentals when coaching youth basketball, it is imperative that you build a solid foundation of basic skills that will allow players to not only develop those skills, but also build confidence in their ability to play basketball. This confidence in turn assists them in developing a love for, and an appreciation of, the game of basketball. The fundamentals, which are individual- and team-based, include playing (motor or movement) skills, plus mental and emotional skills. This chapter focuses on individual skills the players will need to be successful in basketball.

Motor Skills

- Footwork
  - ✓ Stance—the basic position of quickness and balance for basketball movement
  - ✓ Starts—for offense and defense
  - ✓ Steps—running forward and backward, changing direction, and making V cuts
  - ✓ Turns—front and rear pivots
  - ✓ Jumps—from one foot and from two feet

Teach motor skills

- Ballhandling
  - ✓ Passing (chest, overhead, push, baseball)—the basic air and bounce passes used in the game of basketball
  - ✓ Catching (two-hand, one-hand block and tuck)
  - ✓ Dribbling (low, high, change sides)
- Shooting
  - ✓ Set/jump shot (two- and three-point field goals)
  - ✓ Lay-up—close shots from one foot or both feet
  - ✓ Free throw
- Rebounding—gaining possession of the ball after a shot
  - ✓ Capturing and protecting the ball
  - ✓ Offense
  - ✓ Defense
- Individual Defense
  - ✓ Stance
  - ✓ Steps (slide, run, or sprint)
  - ✓ On-ball (live ball, situation, defending a dribbler)
  - ✓ Off-ball (closed, open stances)
  - ✓ On-ball to off-ball situations—jumping to the ball
  - ✓ Off-ball to on-ball (closeouts)
  - ✓ Post defense—defending a player close to the basket when he positions himself with his back toward the basket

- Special skills
  - ✓ Getting open (V cuts)
  - ✓ Setting and using screens—getting a teammate open by screening for them
  - ✓ Pass and cut/give and go—a basic play between two offensive teammates
  - ✓ Posting up (back to basket)—getting open close to the basket as an inside or post player
  - ✓ Perimeter player skills—offensive skills used when facing the basket

Mental/Emotional Skills

Attitude

Attitude is an individual trait that is totally under individual control. A positive attitude is essential for enjoyment and learning, as well individual and team success. Teach players to "take charge of," and be responsible for, their attitude. They must focus on what is best for the team (first) and themselves (second). Many experts consider attitude to be the most important mental/emotional skill.

Mistake Mentality

Learning is enhanced when you allow mistakes to occur and use them to foster improvement. Mistakes are necessary for learning. Use them as status reports for

Teach emotional skills

progress. Teach players that mistakes are okay, and that they should use them and attempt to reduce them in number. They must also avoid effort-related mistakes and making the same mistakes over and over. The challenge for you is to develop a mistake mentality that uses mistakes as tools for learning the game and avoids developing a fear of making mistakes.

Love of the Game

Players need to learn to enjoy and meet the satisfying challenges of basketball. Their participation in a voluntary, fun, and enjoyable atmosphere of play and competition can foster a love of basketball. To enhance this love, give players responsibility (i.e., empower them), hold them accountable for their actions, and treat all players with dignity and respect. An emphasis on developing a love of the game when coaching youth basketball helps players build close relationships with teammates as well as coaches.

Self-Control

It is important that players learn to be emotional and fully involved without losing control. Children's ability to do so will depend in large part on the example set by coaches. The fun and enjoying challenges of basketball are good tests of self-control. Encourage players to be enthusiastic without going overboard. Extreme instances of out-of-control players need to be addressed with corrections, time-outs, and, in rare cases, punishment consequences after a warning. Players need to control not only their attitude, but also their actions and reactions.

Encourage and develop mental skills

Success

Define success in terms of each player doing his best. Hall of Fame Coach John Wooden states that, "Success is peace of mind, which is a direct result of self-satisfaction in knowing you did your best to become the best that you are capable of becoming." Players and teams that focus on this kind of success tend to feel good about their participation, regardless of wins and losses. They tend to focus on the present and enjoy each moment as they practice and play. This is a valuable life lesson for all to learn: Do your best to become your best, on and off the floor.

9

Behavioral Expectations

"Every person has complete control over his attitudes, actions, and responses."
—Jerry Krause, Hall of Fame Coach

Defining an Athletic Attitude

Positive attitudes come from positive experiences. Each player must have a positive belief about the game, the team, and himself. Attitude is a choice, but it often has to be taught and molded. Once you have built the foundation by teaching your athletes about how to make the proper choices, players at any age can be held accountable for the attitudes they display. Most young players will join your team without a clear understanding of what a "good attitude" is. An athletic attitude must be clearly defined, taught, expected, and assessed. As a rule, attitudes are much more within your control than the talent level of your athletes. Therefore, attitude development should be an area of focus throughout the year. Sports are voluntary (both to play and to coach) and no one should be forced into playing. Likewise, effort and attitude are also voluntary. They are choices that each individual can commit to on his own. At the conclusion of the athletic experience, a good attitude will be more helpful than any basketball skill.

For the athlete to properly learn about attitude, he needs clear vision and positive-demanding models. Knowing exactly what behaviors are going to be accepted and what behaviors are not will help every player. It is up to you to make the difference

Attitude is taught and learned

clear early and often during the season. Describe in detail exactly what "attitude" means on your team, and define each descriptive word—effort, poise, unselfishness, etc. Once the terms are defined, athletes will see why having an "athletic attitude" is essential for individual and team success. Talent alone will only take a team so far. The combination of learned skills (based on ability) and attitude is what allows a team to enjoy the experience of reaching its potential. Negativism and bad attitudes are contagious and undermine the motives, strategies, and covenants of the team, and also take the joy out of the game for both players and coaches. Having a positive attitude is a choice that everyone can make on a daily basis, and you need to generously reaffirm, endorse, and praise the character traits over which the team has complete *control—effort* and *attitude*. A positive athletic attitude should be a requirement for being part of your team. The attitude of a team is the clearest reflection of its leadership.

Attitude

Bruce Brown—Hall of Fame Coach

Understand and model the core covenants of the team. Be aggressive, enthusiastic, confident, and disciplined, and compete fearlessly. Be intelligent enough to listen and develop the ability to work and learn. Have faith in the people you are working with. Don't let your teammates down and always put the team ahead of yourself. Maintain integrity and your sense of humor.

Defining the Key Concepts Behind "Attitude"

Core Covenants

A covenant is a binding agreement in which you can see visible action. It is what you and your team stand for. It contains your cornerstones, identity, and guiding principles. Covenants are nonnegotiable on great teams. An example might be to become a "blue collar" team with a great work ethic.

Aggressiveness

Athletics should be played aggressively, within the rules. It is always best to be the individual or team that is on the attack. Do not prepare or play cautiously or nervously. Mental aggressiveness is as important as physical aggressiveness. Being mentally aggressive entails approaching everything as a positive, looking forward to challenges, and quickly recovering from personal mistakes or mistakes of the team.

Enthusiasm

Enthusiasm is both powerful and contagious. It provides energy for athletes to be better workers and improve more quickly. It is okay for players and coaches to let people know that they love the game and the team. Remind your players that it is difficult to excel in anything that you don't love. An enthusiastic athlete puts his heart in his work and is not embarrassed to let it show. He can start his own engine and comes to practices and games with his motor running and ready to be at his best.

Confidence

True confidence is based on preparation. Success, accomplishment, and productive preparation build confidence. It is not built through pep talks. Coaches and teammates can provide steady, positive reinforcement of things done well and constructively criticize things that need improvement. Confidence is mostly spread through your example. You must demonstrate many things very quickly to your team, the most obvious being that you are fully prepared. Do not be nervous. Instead, eagerly anticipate every game and practice. You can help prepare players for competition by reminding them of times when they have performed well. Also, remind them of the confidence you have in them based on their effort to prepare. Confident athletes will challenge themselves in practices to do things they can't do... yet.

Do not ask your players to do things in a game that they have not been able to do in practice. When you hear a coach say "play within yourself," he is really asking his players to only do the things that they know they can accomplish in game situations and that they have demonstrated successfully in practice. Another key concept behind confidence is the ability to learn to compete against your own best self (or team) and not against an opponent. As a coach, you should have a vision of how good your team can become and then coach against that vision. Keep the focus on playing against the vision and not against any given opponent. This allows for winning or losing without the scoreboard.

> *A team that wins on the scoreboard but doesn't perform the way they had practiced, does not really win, but a team that loses on the scoreboard and did everything to the best of their ability and as performed in practice, in truth, has won.*

Discipline

Discipline is involved in all team success. Athletically, discipline is best defined as focused attention and effort, which allows an individual to do what he has been trained to do—as well as possible, each and every time. Discipline fosters a team trust—"I can depend on you." Individual and collective sacrifices involving discipline must be made for a team to be successful. An athlete and teammate must not only accept discipline, but embrace it for the benefit of the group. Disciplined athletes do whatever is necessary concerning work habits, enthusiasm, controlled emotion, and personal responsibility. Great competitors find a way to channel their emotions and energy to lift their own performance, as well as that of the team. Discipline entails training and choices that make punishment unnecessary and focused performance possible.

Competitive Fearlessness

Expect your teams to compete fearlessly, not fearfully or carelessly. Teams that compete fearlessly have prepared as well as possible and react correctly to mistakes. Competing fearlessly requires mental toughness. A mentally tough athlete stays positive, enthusiastic, and confident, no matter what happens. His spirit cannot be broken. He understands that mistakes made at full speed and with full attention are okay, and he can quickly forgive not only his teammates, but also himself. Players should think *WIN* (*w*hat's *i*mportant *n*ow). In other words, players must get over what just happened and get on with the next play. Competing fearlessly is one of the greatest experiences an athlete can have and the ability to do so is among the greatest gifts a coach can give.

Ability to Listen

Anything you can do as a coach to get your athletes to listen completely is worth doing. Get and maintain the absolute attention of your athletes. Without attentiveness, no improvement can take place. Expect your athletes to look directly at the person who is speaking—with both their eyes and their ears. Develop an "attention getter"—a whistle or signal of some kind that lets your players know that you need their attention immediately. Quick attentiveness saves teaching and practice time. Develop a teaching style that allows you to quickly get your players' attention, give quick instructions, and then get them quickly back to action.

Work Ethic

An athlete should be expected to display excellent work habits. Remind your players that their success will always be a direct by-product of their work ethic. Teams are most successful when athletes prepare hard every day. When success does come to them, they should attribute it back to their preparation. Teams that learn to attribute success to preparation become better and have more true confidence. Hard work should become a standard, and a core covenant of the team. It should define "who they are" as athletes and a team. By keeping your focus and reinforcement on controllable factors like work habits, you can hold the standards extremely high. No one on a great team is exempt from exhibiting excellent work habits, including you. You must also make the effort to be the best you can be, every day. Your most talented players need to be the best examples of work ethic the team has. The degree of preparation and the intensity of work expected are two aspects of sport over which you have complete control. Remind your athletes that work, concentration, and effort are choices.

Ability to Learn

Every athlete should work to develop a teachable spirit, and be constantly willing to learn and attempting to improve. Being "coachable" means that the athlete has learned to accept correction as a compliment. Remind your athletes that your corrections mean that you believe in them, that you think that they have the ability to get better. Otherwise, why bother providing correction? When corrected, an athlete should be expected to look at the person who is doing the correcting and respond with a "Thanks, coach."

Faith in People

A collective responsibility exists on motivated teams. Each team member senses this team responsibility and acts with a collective spirit. They win together and they lose together. In an effort to truly become responsible, team members need to fully accept the relatively simple premise that the group can accomplish more together than any one individual could ever hope to achieve alone.

One of the primary roles of leadership is to build a level of trust and mutual respect among all members of the team. The ability to build a diverse group into a complementary team that uses the individual strengths of the athletes and protects any players' weaknesses is of the utmost importance. The greatest compliment between teammates is to be able to be counted on, accountable, and trusted. Teach your athletes to work with, and for, each other. Another measure of faith is when the athletes learn to trust their training, which means that they trust, respect, and depend on the instruction they have received from you. Faith and trust allow teams to get through times when things are going poorly.

Reliability

This concept needs to be the foundation for collective motivation. It can be used as a standard for all decisions that an athlete makes over the course of the season. Tell your players, "Don't let your teammates down when it comes to your attention, effort, eligibility, or decisions away from the team."

Placement of Team Ahead of Self

The team should come first in all decisions. One of the fundamental responsibilities of successful team leadership is the elimination of selfishness. Selfishness on the team level or with any individual player will destroy the team faster than anything else. A "team-first" attitude allows people to accept roles that make others better. Great teams have individual players who each make their own unique contribution to the group's success. Players should be expected to be unselfish with effort and with roles. Every decision should be based on the question, "What does the team need from me?"

Personal Integrity

You must model integrity and expect it from every athlete. People with pure intentions do not compromise or waver from their core values. Each athlete's word should be good and he should take responsibility for all of his own choices. His actions should reflect his beliefs and standards. A person of integrity can be trusted because he will do what is right regardless of the consequence or cost. For young athletes, one of the tests of integrity is how they respond when they think no one is watching.

Sense of Humor

A sense of humor keeps athletic competition in perspective. Don't ever let things get so serious that enjoyment cannot be expressed and sincerely humorous situations cannot be enjoyed. Expect your athletes to have fun and to let that enjoyment show.

Dealing with Specific Motivation Problems and Situations

The Unmotivated Player

- Signs
  - ✓ Appears unsure of himself or uncomfortable
  - ✓ May have pressure from someone else to play
  - ✓ Plays for reasons other than love for the game
  - ✓ May appear lazy
  - ✓ Exhibits body language that says he is not interested
  - ✓ Displays inconsistent behavior
  - ✓ Has a short attention span or gets disinterested
  - ✓ Appears that he really doesn't want to be there
  - ✓ Comes unprepared
  - ✓ Comes late
- Suggestions
  - ✓ Ask both the player and the parents (separately) why he is playing. If he is playing only because his parents want him to, either he needs to stop playing or change his priorities so that he is playing for himself or the enjoyment of the experience.
  - ✓ Find the source of hesitance and decide if it is something that can be helped or changed.
  - ✓ Find his hot button, or what turns him on.
  - ✓ Look for, and build on, small successes.
  - ✓ See if you can fulfill his needs and reasons for playing.
  - ✓ Find a role he can accomplish and make him feel like he is contributing and wanted.
  - ✓ Poor performance is not always a sign of a lack of motivation. In most cases, it means that the athlete may have achieved the highest level of skill they are capable of obtaining at this age and, in some cases, no amount of effort or motivation will take him further at this point until he learns to enjoy the game. Focus on one small thing at a time that is enjoyable to the player. Setting an achievable goal, working hard to meet it, and reaching it can produce player satisfaction.
  - ✓ Give an award for the most enthusiastic player—Big Heart Award, Start Your Own Engine Award, Best Encourager Award.

The Fear-of-Failure Player

- Signs
  - ✓ Is not sure he wants to play
  - ✓ Doesn't like to make mistakes in front of anyone
  - ✓ Makes half effort, token effort, or inconsistent effort
  - ✓ Always seems to be injured
  - ✓ Is quick with excuses
  - ✓ Worries or pretends not to care prior to competition
  - ✓ Has no confidence or is overconfident, but guarded
  - ✓ Chooses to not put forth full effort, so that people will say, "If he really tried, he would be good." If he gave full effort and failed, then others would know that he didn't have the ability. He would rather be thought of as "good if he tried" than really find out what his best effort would produce, or that his best effort isn't "good" enough.
  - ✓ May be highly motivated, but is afraid that public "failure" will destroy his self-worth
  - ✓ Emphasizes comparative performance, instead of learning, improving, and doing his best
  - ✓ Is lethargic
  - ✓ Hesitates to make decisions
  - ✓ Usually only gets excited when the outcome goes his way
  - ✓ Plays fearfully or as if the game doesn't matter
  - ✓ Is often discouraged from even entering into competition
  - ✓ Is a new teammate, or someone who is not sure where he stands with the team or coach
  - ✓ Fears success, because people will expect him to repeat it
- Suggestions
  - ✓ External pressure may be causing the problem. Watch to see if the behavior only comes out when certain people are present or watching.
  - ✓ Lack of confidence often comes from fear that the competition will require more than the athlete is capable of doing. Teach your athletes to "play within themselves."
  - ✓ Tell the player to "become an active participant in his own rescue." Give specific suggestions to the player and ensure that he carries them out.
  - ✓ If the player's sense of self is weak, help him to build it up.

✓ Help the athlete identify where the fear is coming from. If fear is too strong, it can paralyze performance.

✓ Reevaluate and reinforce the definition of success based on athlete-controlled and athlete-owned factors, not the scoreboard. Many young people have been influenced to think that winning on the scoreboard always equals success, while losing always equals failure. Therefore, for them to see themselves as "worthy and valuable," they must win. Some young athletes would rather not try than to risk "failure." You and the team parents must get the young athletes to focus on their own best effort and preparation as opposed to comparison to others.

✓ Reward effort, attitude, preparation, and a willingness to take on new challenges. Define these attributes as "success."

✓ Give an award to the Most Fearless Competitor.

The Inattentive Athlete

- Signs
  ✓ Is easily distracted and usually distracts others
  ✓ Talks while you are talking
  ✓ Usually needs extra explanations
  ✓ Leaves instructional sessions not sure where to go or what to do
  ✓ Looks away and allows his eyes to wander when he is being talked to
  ✓ Has to ask others what he is supposed to be doing
- Suggestions
  ✓ When any player is not completely listening, stop what you are saying and wait in silence until all eyes and ears are focused on you and your words.
  ✓ This player may be a completely visual learner and words don't have much meaning—but remind him that he still needs to be focused and attentive.
  ✓ If the inattentiveness continues, isolate the player away from the group. Finish with your instructions and then go deal with the inattentiveness.
  ✓ If you want your players' attention, talk softly.
  ✓ Don't repeat yourself. If players know you will give the instructions again and again, they won't listen the first time.
  ✓ Have an attention-getter—a quick signal (whistle or hand signal) that tells your team that they need to gather quickly around you and listen.
  ✓ Align your players so they are not facing anything that could be a distraction.
  ✓ If the problem persists, eliminate the player for the drill or the practice.
  ✓ Give an award to the Best Listener or Most Attentive Athlete.

The Player New to an Existing Team

- Signs
  - ✓ Not sure where he stands with the group and doesn't know his role
  - ✓ Is unsure
  - ✓ Is nervous
  - ✓ Doesn't want to look silly in front of the others
  - ✓ Stands back and is hesitant

Parents and coaches teach behavior

- Suggestions
- ✓ Meet with the new player before he is introduced to the team.
- ✓ Get him connected with team standards, expectations, etc.
- ✓ Connect him with several key players if possible before practice starts.
- ✓ Teach your existing team how to welcome a new teammate, to be the first to reach out, to hold back criticism, and to give extra time for him to catch up.
- ✓ Have your stronger players work with him to catch up.
- ✓ Be willing to spend extra time with the new player.
- ✓ Find a role that he can play as soon as possible.
- ✓ Reinforce the core covenants with verbal praise.
- ✓ See if the player brings something new to the team, and give recognition for it.

The Slow-Recovery Player

- Signs
  - ✓ Lets mistakes stay with him and affect his future performance
  - ✓ Often makes the same type of mistake
  - ✓ Makes two mistakes in a row
  - ✓ Allows one mistake to last too long
  - ✓ Pouts after mistakes
  - ✓ Gives up easily
  - ✓ Needs constant validation
  - ✓ Is more dramatic than he needs to be
- Suggestions
  - ✓ Any person who chooses to play basketball needs to learn "quick-recovery skills." Teach and constantly reinforce these skills in practice.
  - ✓ Do not allow players to whine, pout, sulk, or make excuses—remove players who do so.
  - ✓ Teach players that the only way to improve is to make mistakes at full speed and with full attention. Mistakes made under these circumstances are valuable and required for growth.
  - ✓ Verbally reinforce mistakes made at full effort and with full attention
  - ✓ Remind this player that mistakes allow for improvement and that allowing a mistake (their own or a teammate's) to continue to affect performance is a selfish decision that adversely affects the entire team.
  - ✓ Different games require different recovery speeds. In a game like golf, an athlete may have five to 10 minutes between shots to compose himself and get refocused, but in basketball and other "continuous-action" sports, the recovery time has to be almost immediate. Teach your players that recovery time must be quick.
  - ✓ If an athlete chooses to play a quick-recovery sport like basketball, he owes it to his team to become a quick-recovery player. The only other choice is to be removed from the game until player recovers from the mistake (and neither the coach nor the player wants to use that technique).
  - ✓ As a last resort, if a player is not responding to positive reinforcement or cannot buy into the importance of his recovery to the team, then you may have to tell him that the only choice he has left you with is to remove him from the game for the length of time it takes him to recover. "When you can't recover from a mistake immediately, let's have you come out for whatever time period is required for you to completely recover."
  - ✓ Give a WIN Award (what's important now) to the player who never lets his mistakes or teammates' mistakes affect his effort or concentration. The award

winner should be someone who recovers quickly and also helps others recover quickly—someone who doesn't get discouraged.

The Selective Participant

- Signs
  - ✓ Is someone who was born with some talent and somewhere along the way has been allowed to think that his talent is enough and can be used "selectively"
  - ✓ Listens selectively—when he feels like it
  - ✓ Chooses when to work and when to coast
  - ✓ Always looks for short cuts and likes days off or easy practices
  - ✓ Gets absorbed in his own agenda—all that matters is what he gets out of the game
  - ✓ Always seems to find a reason to come late or leave early
  - ✓ Seems to find a way out of the difficult parts of practice, but is always ready to show what he can do when the game comes
  - ✓ Sees roles as limiting
- Suggestions
  - ✓ Teach your players to recognize this behavior and see how selfish and detrimental it is to the team.
  - ✓ Teach this player to control his attitude, actions, and responses.
  - ✓ Teach that this behavior is unacceptable to team standards.
  - ✓ Correctly confront (private, direct, immediate, correction) all efforts that are not acceptable.
  - ✓ Publicly praise an athlete when he is making the right behavioral choices and exhibiting a high level of effort.
  - ✓ Teach and reinforce that effort and determination are more important than skill.
  - ✓ After the expectations are clear, look for patterns of half-efforts and be willing to confront or remove a player.
  - ✓ If the "selective participation" doesn't change, eliminate the player for short periods of times and then increase the time as needed (five minutes, a drill, a practice, etc.)
  - ✓ Start your best workers in practice, regardless of talent, until the whole team is made up of good workers.
  - ✓ Eventually, make your decisions based on what is best for the team.
  - ✓ Give an award for the Best Practice Player, Best Worker, and/or Best Teammate.

The "Bad Attitude" Player

- Signs
  - ✓ Exhibits behaviors that are unacceptable according to the team standards
  - ✓ Interferes with teammates' right to learn or the coaches' right to teach
- Suggestions
  - ✓ Write a clear, concise definition of what a "positive athletic attitude" looks like for your team. The clearer it is, the better chance your athletes will rise to the standards.
  - ✓ Develop an "example" file of good and bad attitude choices to use in your coaching.
  - ✓ Attitude is a choice, and the choice can be taught. It is up to you to teach it.
  - ✓ Once positive attitudes have been learned and modeled, they becomes contagious.
  - ✓ Let players know ahead of time what behaviors will not be acceptable, and then *follow through* with your actions.
  - ✓ Hold your athletes accountable for a positive athletic attitude. Keep working with them and try not to give up.
  - ✓ Look for what is causing this behavior and work to correct the cause. What sets him off?
  - ✓ Become skilled and confident in confronting behaviors that are not acceptable. The test is, does the behavior change?
  - ✓ Publicly and generously praise, reaffirm, and endorse athletes when they are making the right behavioral choices.
  - ✓ If the attitude doesn't change, eliminate the player for short period of times and then increase the time as needed.
  - ✓ Eventually, make your decisions based on what is best for the team.
  - ✓ Give a Great Team Attitude Award.

The Quick Learner/Gifted Athlete

- Signs
  - ✓ Easily bored
  - ✓ Always ready for more
  - ✓ *Note*: This player is not usually a problem unless he is bored (as indicated by acting out or being a distraction) or acts like he is "better than his teammates" or "above" them.

- Suggestions
  - ✓ Teach to the level of the fastest learners, while still showing value to the whole team and those who do not learn as quickly.
  - ✓ Spend pre- and postpractice time working with fast and slow learners.
  - ✓ Let this player know that you may be more demanding of him to take him to a higher level. He also needs to know that it may appear that you are being "tougher" on him, or at least "coaching him differently."
  - ✓ Provide challenges and extra incentives to help this player improve, regardless how he compares to others.
  - ✓ Teach him to accept the teammates who are not as gifted and recognize their value to the team.
  - ✓ Teach him to understand that a variety of learning speeds exist on a team, and to accept every player as a good teammate.
  - ✓ If he is a good worker, use him as an example in drills.
  - ✓ Demand great work habits from him.
  - ✓ Have him go first in line.
  - ✓ Recognize that this athlete (like all others) needs his share of encouragement.
  - ✓ Give an award that recognizes the teammate who has been the most helpful to others in the learning process. The most gifted athletes should improve the team by teaching others.

The Slow Learner

- Signs
  - ✓ Tries, but seldom understand anything on the first explanation
  - ✓ Takes extra time
  - ✓ Is never quite sure where to be or what to do when drills start
- Suggestions
  - ✓ Obviously, not all athletes learn at the same pace. To accommodate all ability and learning styles, be ready to provide extra time and alternate ways to learn to some of your team members.
  - ✓ Some players may be able to come to practice a little earlier to get extra assistance, or they may learn from written material.
  - ✓ Ask his parents about his learning style and what you can do to allow for success. Ask the parents how their child is motivated and how he learns best, and then adapt your style to fit his needs.

Most athletes are visual learners—provide them with a video of the skill done correctly. Some athletes may learn and understand faster if they read the material—provide them with written explanations, descriptions, and diagrams.

✓ Athletes and coaches need to understand that providing extra help is another way of saying "I value you as a person and as a team member."

✓ A slower learner must be encouraged and valued when he is willing to ask for help. No athlete can be afraid to ask for help. Never embarrass or discourage a willing learner.

✓ When introducing complex concepts, give this athlete more time.

✓ Consider giving him the new information the day before.

✓ Pair a slower learner up with a patient, more skilled player for new drills.

✓ Place him in a spot where an assistant coach is nearby and ready to help.

✓ Be aware of the competitive situations you put him in during practice. You must be able to build one player's confidence without reducing another player's confidence.

✓ Give an award that reinforces perseverance in learning new skills.

The Overconfident Athlete

- Signs (overconfidence is only a problem if these behaviors surface)
  ✓ Brags
  ✓ Carries himself with a swagger
  ✓ Has a "better-than-you" attitude
  ✓ Displays a taunting, "I can coast and still beat you," or an "I already know everything" attitude
  ✓ Disrespects teammates, opponents, or coaches
  ✓ Criticizes others
  ✓ Demonstrates a sense of entitlement
- Suggestions
  ✓ Teach your athletes to differentiate between true confidence (quiet confidence based upon preparation) and arrogance.
  ✓ Confidence becomes a problem only when it is displayed in a style that demonstrates disrespect for others or to the point where an individual player does not perform as well as possible.

✓ If the problem persists, try to show the overconfident athlete proper perspective. But be careful when trying to teach humility. Don't humble the player to the point where he loses a valuable level of confidence. When working with athletes who would benefit themselves and the team by being humbled, first attempt to do it privately. Make sure that he is strong enough, do it carefully, and then build him back up after you have gotten his attention. Instead of using personal criticism, try to use examples that clearly show why the behavior is not acceptable.

✓ Getting the player to actually see offensive behavior through the eyes of a teammate or opponent is important. Use game or practice videos to alert him to how his words or actions can be seen as negative, hurtful, or simply unacceptable behavior.

✓ Teach humility in victory and graciousness in defeat. Some athletes who appear to be overconfident are really just covering up for insecurities.

✓ Give an award that recognizes Quiet Confidence.

Low-Confidence Athlete

- Signs
  ✓ Exhibits shyness
  ✓ Is fragile—sensitive to all correction, especially in front of others
  ✓ Is unwilling to try at times
  ✓ Looks for validation
  ✓ Fears your reaction and looks to the bench or the stands after he has made a mistake
  ✓ Hates to perform/fail in front of anyone
- Suggestions
  ✓ Develop a player-coach relationship that encourages trust.
  ✓ Stay calm and do not make any loud or quick reactions to mistakes.
  ✓ Be careful and use words, inflections, and actions that are patient, reassuring, and supportive.
  ✓ Build on any small success.
  ✓ Help this player focus on the physical or mental adjustments that need to be made to improve performance—not on the final outcome.
  ✓ Teach the connection between real confidence and preparation.
  ✓ Get the focus off outcome and the scoreboard and keep it on preparation.

The Angry Athlete

- Signs
  - ✓ Has a bad temper/outbursts
  - ✓ Reacts quickly and negatively when things don't go his way
  - ✓ Gets frustrated easily
  - ✓ Wants to argue and blame others
  - ✓ Pouts
  - ✓ Uses anger to motivate himself
- Suggestions
  - ✓ Learn to identify the fine line between aggressiveness and anger.
  - ✓ As the coach, *model the poise you expect your athletes to display*.
  - ✓ Teach this athlete how frustration usually deflates his teammates and encourages the opponents—the exact opposite of what a real competitor wants to do.
  - ✓ Some frustration can be okay if it doesn't detract from a player's physical performance or behavior as a teammate. It is not good if it lasts too long or interferes with the performance of the individual or team.
  - ✓ Take the athlete out of the game and be an example of calm.
  - ✓ Provide a reminder (cue or key) that you can use with the athlete during a game or at practice to prevent and control anger.
  - ✓ Provide a method for the player to refocus and give him a time limit to become poised and focused. One method might be to talk to a calm teammate.
  - ✓ Remind this player that anger, frustration, and temper are selfish behaviors if they affect the team in a negative manner.
  - ✓ Teach all athletes to keep their focus where it belongs—on their assignment, the next play, and the team—*not* on opponents or officials.
  - ✓ Give an award for the Most Poised Athlete.

10

Daily Character Lessons
for Youth Basketball

"Your reputation is what others think you are. Your character is what you truly are."
—John Wooden, Naismith Hall of Fame Player and Coach

It is essential that you incorporate lessons of character into your daily practice plans. Character can be taught, learned, and improved at almost any age. You can take the character lessons into as much depth as time and the age of your team allow. Begin by identifying the level of teaching that best fits your athletes' age group. Your lessons should be divided into the five core values of the NAIA Champions of Character Program. Each of these core values is divided into sections as follows:

- Definition—teach one sentence or one concept at a time
- Choices to which the athlete can commit
- Questions for the athlete or team to discuss or write about

Make your expectations and values clear. Articulate, teach, practice, model, and praise these values on a daily basis to provide an experience during which athletes can learn and demonstrate exactly what it means to be an athlete and person of character.

Young athletes should be able to learn and demonstrate how to:
- Be reliable when it comes to listening, being on time, and being completely focused
- Take correction without making excuses or deflecting blame
- Keep promises and finish what they start

- Understand that temper is not part of playing or being a competitor
- Tell the truth and play within the rules and the spirit of the game
- Help others
- Win with humility and lose with dignity
- Understand the value of rules
- Be part of a team and not always get their own way
- Develop some leadership skills
- Attribute all of these lessons to the appropriate values and become a person of character

The primary purpose of coaching is to use sports to teach athletes to become better people. Viewing coaching as an opportunity to hold your athletes to the highest possible behavioral standards is what gives the profession eternal value. Players will not come to you with all of these character-related attributes in place, but every child has the capacity to learn and be good. Athletics offers one of the best chances outside the family for young people to learn responsibility, respect, integrity, sportsmanship, and servant leadership (or vice-versa). Coaching is an awesome opportunity to impact the lives of young people.

The five values of the NAIA Champions of Character Program are as follows:
- Responsibility—Learning to be accountable and disciplined
- Respect—Learning to work and to develop the right kind of confidence
- Integrity—Learning to do what is right—actions must match words
- Sportsmanship—Learning to respect the spirit of the game
- Servant Leadership—Becoming a team player and leader, which entails developing an attitude of service to the people you lead and serving others on your team as you lead yourselves in a responsible manner.

Responsibility

An athlete can demonstrate responsibility in two ways: accountability and discipline.

Accountability

Pregame Reminders

Athletes have a responsibility to be accountable, which entails taking ownership of whatever happens to them. Accountability builds trust between teammates. A player can become known for being reliable and for being someone others can count on when it comes to work that must be performed. Reliability is developed from daily work habits. Great teams have individual members who feel and act with collective responsibility. They win together and they lose together. No excuses are needed because each teammate takes personal responsibility for his mistakes. These players do not want to let each other down. Success individually feels good, but success collectively feels great. Learning to depend on each other and to be dependable makes everyone better. These teams have players who place their personal signature on everything the team does. An atmosphere of trust exists because promises are kept and people are seen as trustworthy. Great teammates must be able to count on each other. Personal character involves being accountable, and being accountable makes trust possible. The greatest compliment a player can receive from a teammate is that he can be counted on.

Game-Time Reminders

Distribute the following checklist to your athletes and ask them to review it periodically to make sure they are staying on track.

As an accountable athlete, I can choose to:
- Follow instructions—when instructions are given, they will be carried out to the best of my ability
- Concentrate on my work
- Not give excuses—I will face problems head on
- Not blame others—I will look to myself first after a mistake
- Understand that consequences exist for all of my actions

Discipline

Pregame Reminders

Athletes have a responsibility to be disciplined. For a true athlete, discipline is not punishment, but rather a positive statement from the coach that he believes the player can do what is best for the team. Discipline is simply focused attention and effort. Being disciplined will result in more productive practices and more purposeful teaching. More will be accomplished when the individuals and the team as a whole are disciplined. Being a disciplined athlete brands a player as reliable, trustworthy, and "coachable." One of the first things that identifies a disciplined athlete is a teachable spirit. The mature athlete has learned to take correction as a compliment, which demonstrates respect for self and the team. An athlete who can take correction as a compliment says with his body language and words, "Thanks for caring enough about me that you think I can improve."

Game-Time Reminders

Distribute the following checklist to your athletes and ask them to review it periodically to make sure they are staying on track.

As a disciplined athlete, I can choose to:
- Always go to practice and prepare properly for games
- Arrive at practice motivated to work, see, listen, and learn
- Have a teachable spirit and take correction as a compliment
- Look at the person who is speaking to me or correcting me
- Listen to my coaches, parents, and teachers
- Earn the respect of everyone

Halftime Reminders

Ask your athletes the following questions about responsibility (i.e., response ability):
- Who is the most trustworthy person you know and why?
- Who is the most disciplined person you know and why?
- What responsibilities do you have to this team?
- What responsibilities do you have to your family?

Postgame Reminders

Post the following quotes to reinforce responsibility:
- "If it is to be, it is up to me." (Frosty Westering)
- "He who is good at making excuses, is seldom good for anything else." (Benjamin Franklin)
- "It is easier to do a job right than to explain why you didn't." (Martin Van Buren)
- "The successful man is the average man, focused." (Unknown)
- "Don't whine, don't complain, and don't make excuses." (John Wooden)

Respect

An athlete can demonstrate respect in two ways: work habits/initiative and true confidence.

Work Habits

Pregame Reminders

An athlete demonstrates respect by developing consistent work habits. One of the most important life lessons that youngsters can learn from sport participation is the ability to work. An athlete who can learn to focus and perform the physical and mental work necessary to be successful can carry this work ethic over into the classroom and eventually to his profession. Good work habits begin with initiative, and are reinforced by success and the building of the true confidence that comes from preparation.

Working hard builds a player's reputation for responsibility and accountability and is sincerely appreciated by teammates. Like other character traits, work becomes who you are (i.e., a good and dependable worker), and proudly spreads to the entire team family. Reliable work habits foster deep and lasting friendship, loyalty, respect, and love.

Game-Time Reminders

Distribute the following checklists to your athletes and ask them to review them periodically to make sure they are staying on track.

As an athlete with initiative, I can choose to:
- Be a self-starter
- Be eager to learn
- Keep my promises
- Not put things off
- Finish what I start

As an athlete who wants to model good work habits, I can choose to:
- Focus for an entire practice without distraction
- Consistently give my best effort

Confidence

Pregame Reminders

An athlete demonstrates respect by understanding and modeling true confidence, which should not ever be confused with arrogance or boisterous behavior. Athletic confidence is more likely to be a quiet confidence, based on preparation that allows the player to concentrate and visualize a positive effort. You must work to break down the so-called confident images of athletes displaying arrogance on TV. Don't let your players confuse confidence with self-centeredness or bragging. Athletes with quiet, inner confidence know that they will perform well based on how they have practiced and prepared.

Game-Time Reminders

Distribute the following checklist to your athletes and ask them to review it periodically to make sure they are staying on track.

As a confident athlete, I can choose to:
- Not draw attention to myself
- Be silent with my boasts
- Know how to shake hands and confidently introduce myself to others

Halftime Reminders

Ask your athletes the following questions about respect:
- What person do you respect most and why?
- Who is the hardest worker you know?
- Which athlete have you seen that has respectful confidence?
- How can you earn and demonstrate respect to your team? To your opponents?
- How can you earn and demonstrate respect to your family?

Postgame Reminders

Post the following quotes to reinforce respect:
- "The harder you work, the harder it is to surrender." (Vince Lombardi)
- The six W's—"Work will win when wishing won't." (Todd Blackledge)
- "When I was young, I never wanted to leave the court until I got things exactly correct." (Larry Bird)
- "Don't confuse activity with achievement." (John Wooden)
- "Start your own engine." (Tim Driver)
- "A job well begun is half done." (Proverb)
- "Earn respect yourself and give respect to others." (Jerry Krause)

Learning respect

Integrity

Integrity is a set of behaviors displayed through small daily decisions. The athlete demonstrates actions that follow his words and beliefs. His core covenants and his behavior align. His "yes" means yes and his "no" means no. The athlete of integrity says what he means and follows that exact path. His word is good, his handshake confirms the deal, and his signature is worth something. He is worthy of respect. The first step to building a successful team is surrounding yourself with people of integrity.

Integrity is a simple concept, and life may not be any easier for the person of integrity, but it is simpler. It is not always easy to do what is ethically correct, but it is simple to know which path is most ethical and then exercise that option.

Game-Time Reminders

Distribute the following checklist to your athletes and ask them to review it periodically to make sure they are staying on track.

As an athlete of integrity, I can choose to:
- Tell the truth
- Admit when I am wrong
- Understand cheating and refuse to break the rules of the game
- Not take advantage of the rules for personal gain
- Honor my team and my family with my actions

Halftime Reminders

Ask your athletes the following questions about integrity:
- Who is a person of integrity in your life and how does he demonstrate it?
- What does a team of integrity look like?
- If you have to cheat to win, do you really win?
- How can you demonstrate integrity in your family?

Postgame Reminders

Post the following quotes to reinforce integrity:
- "The true test of character is not how much we know how to do, but how we behave when we don't know what to do." (John Holt)
- "He who permits himself to lie once, finds it much easier to do it a second and third time, until it becomes a habit." (Thomas Jefferson)

- "Integrity is telling myself the truth." (Samuel Johnson)
- "Outside show is a poor substitute for inner worth." (Aesop)
- "Don't lie, cheat, or steal." (John Wooden)

Sportsmanship

Pregame Reminders

Sportsmanship is a positive reaffirmation of the fact that an athlete is disciplined enough to have perspective, maintain poise, and do what is best for his teammates. Sportsmanship is not a passive activity of acceptance. It is a choice. Being able to make the correct behavioral choice at the "moment of truth" is a responsibility that comes with choosing to be part of a team. Character is often best revealed in pressure-packed situations.

Game-Time Reminders

Distribute the following checklists to your athletes and ask them to review them periodically to make sure they are staying on track.

As an athlete of character, I can choose to always:
- Respect my opponents
- Respect those in authority (coaches, officials, teachers, parents, etc.)
- Understand the difference between the rules and the "spirit of the game"
- Respect the rules and spirit of the game

I can choose to be an athlete who models sportsmanship by:
- Valuing opponents as necessary to challenge me to do my best
- Refusing to cheer or jeer an opponent's failure
- Helping up a fallen opponent
- Patting an opponent on the back in a gesture of "nice play" or "way to go"
- Courteously handing the ball to, or getting the ball for, the official
- Understanding and demonstrating humility when my team has won
- When shaking or slapping hands at the conclusion of the game, taking my time with at least one of the opposing players to identify something about him that I appreciate or admire instead of just saying "good game"
- Sincerely shaking hands and looking the other person in the eye

As a poised athlete, I can choose to:
- Be someone who offers encouragement when things are bad
- Be slow to lose my temper

Demonstrate sportsmanship

- Always think before I take any action that impacts myself or the team
- Walk away from situations that could be a problem or not good for my team

Halftime Reminders

Ask your athletes the following questions about sportsmanship:
- Is it ever okay to:
    - ✓ Yell and wave your arms during a free throw?
    - ✓ Boo an official's decision?
    - ✓ Display temper with a coach or official's decisions?
    - ✓ Make comments or yell to antagonize opponents?
    - ✓ Make statements that distract or upset opponents? Encourage the team's fans to do the same?
    - ✓ Refuse to shake hands?
    - ✓ Use profanity when you are upset?
    - ✓ Be suckered into a physical or verbal conflict?
- How will you act and look when our team wins?
- How will you act and look when our team loses?
- Is there such a thing as sportsmanship outside of sports?
- How can you demonstrate sportsmanship in your family?

Postgame Reminders

Post the following quotes to reinforce sportsmanship:
- "To win by cheating is not really to win at all. Athletics offers a chance to stand up for what is right." (Pete Dawkins)
- "Athletes should not celebrate insanely when they win, nor sulk when they lose. They should accept victory professionally and humbly, and when defeated, make no poor display of it." (Dan Gable, Olympic Gold Medal Wrestler)
- "An athlete is not crowned unless he competes according to the rules." (II Timothy 2:5)
- "Win with humility and lose with dignity." (John Wooden)

Servant Leadership

An athlete can demonstrate servant leadership in two ways: team-first attitude and leadership.

Team-First Attitude

Pregame Reminders

An athlete of character understands and can demonstrate a team-first attitude. Those athletes in leadership positions understand and can model servant leadership. These athletes always put the needs of the team ahead of their own. Being part of a team involves an intentional step from independence (me first) to interdependence (we first). One of the best examples of being a "we-first" teammate is when a player accepts a role on a team. Choosing to play a game in which multiple roles are necessary for team success is a test of character, commitment, and leadership. A team-first attitude allows people to accept roles that make others better. Great teams have individuals who each make their own unique contribution to the group's success. At least one player needs to have the skills to perform each of the duties necessary for the team to collectively function.

Game-Time Reminders

Distribute the following checklist to your athletes and ask them to review it periodically to make sure they are staying on track.

As a teammate, I can choose to:
- Be part of the team and help others recover after mistakes
- Understand that this team is bigger than me and that I am one important part of it

- Accept the role the coach and team needs me to play
- Not complain when I do not get my own way
- Know that things are not always going to be, or need to be, "fair" from my point of view
- Make teammates feel important
- Say "thanks" when I am helped, "good job" when others succeed, and "let me help" when work needs to get done
- Welcome new people onto the team

Leadership

Pregame Reminders

The best team leaders are the first to serve, putting others before themselves. The servant leader is the one who is the first to volunteer to help and never too proud to do work, even the difficult or unpopular jobs. Those jobs may be done without anyone knowing because no complaining or comparing takes place. The servant leader is reliably and consistently a servant for others on the team.

The team leader is a positive role model for others through his actions and words. His effort is never questioned, his positive enthusiasm is never hidden, and his sportsmanship demonstrates respect to teammates, opponents, and the spirit of the game.

Game-Time Reminders

Distribute the following checklist to your athletes and ask them to review it periodically to make sure they are staying on track.

As an athlete who wants to be a leader, I can choose to:
- Enjoy the successes of my teammates
- Be willing to let others go first, take more turns, or get more attention
- Listen, as well as speak
- Respect others' opinions
- Not take advantage of other people
- Look for ways to help others
- Look for the good in others
- Always put the team above me
- Always build up others without looking for personal recognition
- Strive to be a positive example

Halftime Reminders

Ask your athletes the following questions about servant leadership:
- Who is the best leader you know and why?
- Who do you know that is the best example of a willingness to serve others?
- How can you be both a leader and a servant?
- What is the best team you have been on and why?
- What can you do to serve this team?
- What can you do to serve your family?

Postgame Reminders

Post the following quotes to reinforce servant leadership:
- "The main ingredient in stardom is the rest of the team." (Unknown)
- "The power of we is greater than the power of *me*." (Unknown)
- "The greatest joy one can have is doing something for someone else, without having any thought of getting something in return." (John Wooden)
- "Talent may win games, but teamwork and intelligence win championships." (Michael Jordan)
- "To have a friend, be a friend." (Unknown)
- "A champion team will beat a team of champions." (Unknown)

11

Teaching Tips

"Give a man a fish and you feed him for a day.
Teach a man to fish and you feed him for a lifetime"

—Chinese proverb

The key role of a youth basketball coach is to develop young people through the sport of basketball—physically, mentally/emotionally, and socially. Teaching is a complex skill that depends upon communication and leadership skills. You must master the basics of communication, leadership, and teaching—especially as applied to youngsters in basketball—to teach players to understand, appreciate, and enjoy basketball for a lifetime.

Teaching

When teaching skills and other basketball-related concepts, the most common process is to apply the basic laws of learning: demonstration and explanation; imitation of the demonstration; correction of the imitation with performance feedback; and repetition, repetition, repetition. The games approach (see Appendix C) is an alternative teaching method that allows players to compete/play first to discover the need for certain skills. Afterward, you can follow the basic learning laws before returning to play/competition. Practicing proper performance is essential to learning, growth, and improvement. Practice only makes permanent, not perfect, which makes your feedback that much more critical.

Teach, communicate, and lead

Demonstration of skills must be done correctly, as the young learner must have the essential parts of the skill (i.e., the critical cues) in a mental picture to imitate. You may use one of the better players or a video or DVD to demonstrate a skill. However, it is always better if you can perform the demonstration yourself. Skill demonstration can be learned for nearly all fundamental skills. It adds credibility to your coaching, is very time efficient, and can enhance your confidence. Demonstrations should be done so that every player can clearly see and hear the performance with full attention. Demonstrations also need to be repeated from at least two perspectives. For example, demonstrate with a side view and a front view. Seeing the skill from different angles can enhance learning. Demonstrations can also be performed and repeated at various speeds for clarity.

Each skill demonstration should be accompanied by an explanation that is precise, but also concise. Critical cues, or keys, should be limited to no more than three (less is better), so as to reduce "analysis paralysis" when the young players imitate the skill. See *Basketball Skill Progressions* and the *NABC Basketball Skills & Drills for Younger Players* DVD/video series for examples of critical cues. The idea is to get to the imitation stage quickly after the demonstration is performed—avoid talking players to death. They learn basketball by seeing and doing more than by listening.

Following the demonstration/explanation of the skill, players need to imitate the skill quickly and often. Repetition is needed to improve performance and learning. As a player imitates a skill, he may begin to slowly and gradually increase his speed until he approaches game speed Game moves at game speed is the ultimate goal. When players begin slowly, they should get a rhythm and then go faster and faster until mistakes are made. Mistakes are an indication that learning is taking place. In fact, mistakes are absolutely necessary for learning when using this method. Develop a healthy "mistake mentality" in your players that focuses on full attention and effort. Mistakes will then be viewed as status reports on learning and improvement.

You play a critical role during the imitation stage. You must correct the imitation, primarily by providing informative feedback (critical cues). The most common coaching error during this stage is to focus on what the player is doing wrong (mistakes), when special emphasis is needed on what the player is doing right (praise of critical cues). This feedback should be precise and specific, and be given as soon as possible after the skill is performed.

One way to give feedback is by using what is called Docheff's feedback sandwich (Figure 11-1). The feedback sandwich consists of the following:
- General praise/encouragement of something being done correctly—"Good job of getting your feet ready on the shot."
- Meaty information at the heart of the sandwich, delivered without too much emotion—"You need to have full follow-through on the shot. Shoot up, not out, and fully extend your elbow."

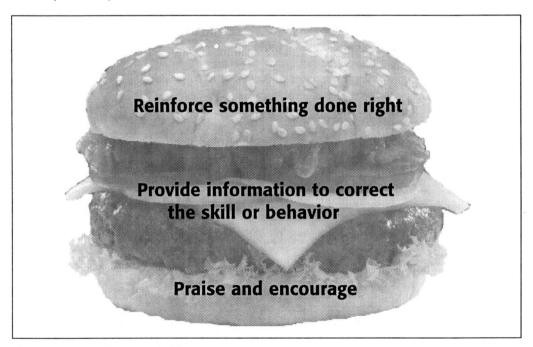

Figure 11-1. Feedback sandwich

- A feedback finish consisting of some form of praise/reinforcement—"Good job. Your shot is getting better and more consistent."

Always accompany correction/criticism with praise. Make the necessary corrections, but also provide praise of correct performance. Know the skills well enough to center on the critical cues and effort, not just on outcome. It is essential that you explain to players that correction/criticism is necessary to enhance learning. Thus, players should treat correction/criticism as the highest compliment. It means you are helping the player get better. Be interested enough to give the learner the proper feedback needed for improvement.

Correcting performance and providing feedback to players is a never-ending task. Remember that players learn by doing, so feedback shouldn't always interrupt practice. Catch them on the move and allow enough repetitions so that learning can take place. Feedback can be less frequent as players improve, but it is always essential. Proceed slowly from having players perform skills in slow motion (correctly), until mistakes are made as each player focuses on attaining "game moves at game speed."

Communication

Teaching requires the use of all communication skills: verbal, nonverbal, listening, reading, writing, and the use of computers. The most challenging areas for most coaches seem to be listening skills and nonverbal communication. It is important that you maintain full eye contact and use positive nonverbal language when speaking and listening. Listen fully with your eyes and ears, and expect the same from your players— it is a sign of respect. Communication skills are further described and demonstrated in Chapter 4 of *Basketball Skill Progressions* and the *NABC Basketball Skills & Drills for Younger Players* video series. Remember, young players learn best through example. What you do will always be more important than what you say. Communicate your enthusiasm and love of the game (and them) through your actions.

Leadership

Your ability to lead a basketball team depends upon several behaviors that every coach can improve, enhance, and emphasize:
- Be an example—Role modeling (general) and skill modeling (demonstrating skills) can be critical tools for leading and learning. Young people actively seek and follow positive role models. Become a positive-demanding coach who teaches/leads in positives (e.g., attitude, actions, and responses) and sets high standards of excellence (not perfection). The challenging aspect of setting a good example is that youngsters follow examples on and off the court at all times.

- Show enthusiasm—This contagious characteristic can be used to convey love of the sport and love of young people. Cherish both and look for ways to exhibit that love in a positive, healthy way.
- Be a model of integrity—Do what you say (be honest) and say what you do (be open and follow through on your commitments).
- Earn and build respect—Earn the respect of all you encounter (players, coaches, officials, parents) and help players build their self-respect and confidence. This confidence will depend upon their regular successes in ever-increasing challenges in a positive sport atmosphere.
- Be a servant leader—Set the example for players to put the team first. Do your best job of coaching and lead your athletes toward doing their best.
- Exhibit responsibility—Be accountable for your actions and lead players to do the same.
- Be a model of sportsmanship—Insist on being good and doing what is right. This means treating all players fairly (but not necessarily equally). This area is an important, possibly unique benefit of the sport experience that can be used to teach life lessons.

As Hall of Fame coach Mike Krzyzewski states, you should "lead from the heart," which requires you to develop your leadership style around your unique personality. Be yourself and be true to yourself.

A

Coaching Checklists

The coaching checklists that you develop must cover the following topics:
- Philosophy
- Preseason
- Practice
- Games
- Program Assistants

Checklist #1: Coaching Philosophy

It is helpful to develop and write down a basic coaching philosophy. This process can provide both a foundation for translating ideas into actions and a time for reflection. The philosophy itself is a short, concise statement of the coaching beliefs that your youth basketball program is based upon. It should include the following six essential areas:
- How to empower and involve players
- A focus on fun and fundamentals
- How to develop players through basketball
- A definition of success for players and the program
- Concepts/practices based on your unique personality
- Technical basketball concepts suited to the motivation level of your team

Checklist #2: Preseason

- Develop and write your personal coaching philosophy
- Form your team:
  - ✓ Determine player eligibility
  - ✓ Establish the time and place for tryouts/squad selection
  - ✓ Establish tryout drills and procedures
  - ✓ Identify participants and collect parent/player information forms
  - ✓ Collect communication information (address, phone numbers, email, medical information, emergency contacts)
  - ✓ Set up a communication tree (phone, email)
  - ✓ Recruit program assistants (coaches, equipment/facilities, managers, food and refreshments)
  - ✓ Collect league/competition information
  - ✓ Perform equipment inventory (needs/checkout)
- Determine goals and objectives
- Obtain parent consent forms
- Complete a parent orientation program, which should include the following:
  - ✓ Parent letter
  - ✓ Expectations of players
  - ✓ Goals and objectives
  - ✓ Philosophy
  - ✓ Equipment
  - ✓ Warnings of inherent risks
  - ✓ Family and emergency contact information
  - ✓ Practice/game/league rules
  - ✓ Parent consent forms
  - ✓ Definition of parents' role
  - ✓ Practice and game schedules
- Review legal duties, which include the following:
  - ✓ Proper planning
  - ✓ Supervision (general and specific)
  - ✓ Safe physical environment
  - ✓ Proper instruction

- ✓ Adequate, proper equipment
- ✓ Matching of athletes for competition
- ✓ Evaluation of players for injury
- ✓ Warnings of inherent risks
- ✓ Emergency plan
- Develop your season plan, which should include the following:
  - ✓ Goals and instructional objectives (skills, knowledge, conditioning, values)
  - ✓ Equipment and facilities
  - ✓ Practices (number, format, content, schedule)
  - ✓ Practice schedule (fundamentals, strategies)
  - ✓ Games (dates, times, locations)
  - ✓ Calendar (preseason, competition season, postseason)
  - ✓ Identification of skills and drills/games to teach those skills; daily themes; character/value lessons
  - ✓ Evaluation (coach, players, team, program)
  - ✓ Age/skill/playing adjustments

Checklist #3: Practice

- Develop written practice plans using the practice plan format in Chapter 4. Also refer to the video *NABC Basketball Skills & Drills for Younger Players: Volume 13—Practicing to Play the Game.*
- Equipment and facilities:
  - ✓ Court reservation
  - ✓ Safety check of the facility (baskets, floor swept, obstructions)
  - ✓ Basketballs (minimum of one for every two players) and ball bag
  - ✓ Water; sanitary cups or individual bottles
  - ✓ Towels
  - ✓ Timing devices
  - ✓ Whistle
- Practice themes/focus
  - ✓ Team/value theme
  - ✓ Skill focus
- Practice teams for the day
- Drills/games selected

- Helper assignments
- Individual player work needed
  - ✓ Prepractice
  - ✓ Postpractice
- Team announcements/reminders
  - ✓ Schedule
  - ✓ Next practice/game
  - ✓ Homework

Checklist #4: Games

In preparation for games, ready your basketball team to face all competition challenges, including the following:

Pregame

- Dressing—Shoes, socks, shorts, and uniform top
- Mental/emotional preparation—Teach and tell the players what to expect and how to prepare for the games (the good, the bad, and the ugly).
- Warm-ups—Five to 15 minutes of fundamental skills to include shooting. Rehearse, develop, and teach the warm-up period to get players used to gradually warming up to game speed.
- Team meeting—Usually takes place before the warm-ups to give final reminders and assure players of success and of fun as a focus
- Team huddling—Focus on a "team" or "value" theme embodied in a word or phrase as players break the huddle (e.g., respect, team, defense).

Game Preparation

- Jump balls—Lineup, positions, and responsibilities
- Team offense(s)
  - ✓ Player-to-player
  - ✓ Zone
  - ✓ Transition (defense to offense)—fast break
  - ✓ Out-of-bounds plays (side, under)
  - ✓ Free throws
- Team defense(s)
  - ✓ Player-to-player

✓ Zone

✓ Transition (offense to defense)—rules, strategy

✓ Out-of-bounds plays

✓ Free throws

Miscellaneous

- Time-outs—Calling, content (get their attention, impart one or two concepts, give more information than emotion)
- Halftime—Recovery, brief message, warm-ups
- Postgame—Cool-down, meeting (review one or two game concepts), assignment/lessons learned. Give players time and space to recover. Focus on the next practice.

Checklist #5: Program Assistants

- Determine/solicit assistants for possible program help areas
  ✓ Assistant coach

  ✓ Team manager (equipment and facilities)

  ✓ Food/refreshments (after games)

  ✓ Other (transportation, scheduling, communication, etc.)
- Develop a task list of responsibilities for each category of program assistant (preseason, practices, games, postseason).
- Conduct a preseason meeting to discuss responsibilities and expectations.
- Conduct a postseason evaluation and write notes of appreciation.

Parent Checklists

Distribute the following checklists to the players' parents and ask them use them to evaluate the youth basketball program.

Checklist #1: Youth Basketball Program Assessment

- The coach/program has a written philosophy statement that:
  - ✓ Is focused on fun and fundamentals
  - ✓ Keeps winning in perspective
  - ✓ Defines success in terms of doing your best
  - ✓ Is centered on player development
  - ✓ Emphasizes treating all players with dignity and respect
- The coach/program provides a safe sport experience:
  - ✓ Physically (teaching, facility, emergency)
  - ✓ Emotionally
- The coach/program ensures player development:
  - ✓ Physically (basic skills, conditioning)
  - ✓ Emotionally (all players are treated with dignity and respect)
  - ✓ Socially (team cohesion and chemistry)
- The coach is prepared to teach:
  - ✓ Young people

- ✓ Basketball skills and strategies
- The coach clarifies coach, player, and parent expectations/roles through:
  - ✓ Written philosophy
  - ✓ Parent orientation
  - ✓ Goals and objectives
  - ✓ Legal duties
  - ✓ Planning evidence
  - ✓ Evaluation and assessments

Checklist #2: Parent Assessment

This evaluation allows parents to clarify and maximize their role to optimize the sport experience for their child.

- Recognize that you want what is best for your child and that, as a parent, you will tend to be somewhat subjective
- Know the coach and the program
  - ✓ Safe physically and emotionally
  - ✓ The players' welfare comes first
  - ✓ All players participate in practices and games
  - ✓ Focus on fun and fundamentals
  - ✓ Athletes first, winning second
- Fully release your child to the coach, the sport, and the program
  - ✓ Recognize that your primary role is to support and encourage
  - ✓ Assist with skill development only when asked
  - ✓ Allow only one instructional voice (the coach) at practice and games
  - ✓ Adopt the same sport goals as your child
  - ✓ Make sure you are on the same page as your child and the coach
  - ✓ Model poise and confidence at all times
- Beware of parent "red flags"
  - ✓ Taking credit for athlete/team successes
  - ✓ Trying to solve all of your athlete's problems
  - ✓ Player looks at you when playing (especially after making mistakes)
  - ✓ Embarrassment, suffering, or celebrating athlete/team outcome
- Give these gifts to your child
  - ✓ Focus on team and not just your child

✓ Give postgame time and space for your child to recover
✓ Encourage and support (e.g., "I love watching you play.")
✓ Choose one sport role and do it well (spectator/parent, coach, official, athlete)

C

Coaching Resources

Books and Printed Materials

American Sport Education Program (2001). *Coaching Youth Basketball*. Champaign, IL: Human Kinetics.

Brown, B. (2002) *101 Youth Basketball Drills and Games*. Monterey, CA: Coaches Choice.

Burnett, D. (2001) *Youth Sports and Self-Esteem: A Guide for Parents*. Springfield, MA: Spalding Sports Library.

Dickinson, A. and Garchow, K. (Eds.). (1992). *Youth Basketball: A Complete Handbook*. Dubuque, IA: Brown & Benchmark.

Faucher, D.G. (2000). *The Baffled Parent's Guide to Coaching Youth Basketball*. Camden, ME: Ragged Mountain Press/McGraw-Hill.

Grawer, R. (2003). *Youth Basketball Skills and Drills* (2nd ed.). Monterey, CA: Coaches Choice.

Kozub, F.M. (May/June 2001). Using task cards to help beginner basketball players self-assess. *Strategies*, 14 (5), 18–22.

Krause, J, Janz, C., and Conn, J. (2003). *Basketball Skill Progressions*. Monterey, CA: Coaches Choice.

Krause, J, Meyer, D. and Meyer, J. (1999). *Basketball Skills & Drills*. Champaign, IL: Human Kinetics.

McCarthy, J.P., Jr. (1996). *Coaching Youth Basketball*. Cincinnati, OH: Betterway Books.

Paye, B. (2001). *Youth Basketball Drills*. Champaign, IL: Human Kinetics.

Associations and Organizations

National Youth Sports Coaches Association (NYSCA)
The NYSCA acts as a training center for volunteer youth sports coaches. It is not only a training resource, but also offers opportunities for continuing education on current issues in sport and coaching ethics.
www.nays.org

North American Youth Sports Institute (NAYSI)
The NAYSI is dedicated to helping teachers, coaches, parents, and other youth leaders interact more effectively with children and sports. The website is an excellent resource by itself, including an interactive section where it is possible to submit a question on anything related to sports, fitness, or recreation. The NAYSI website also produces a newsletter about youth sports.
www.naysi.org

Youth Basketball of America (YBOA)
This organization helps coaches, parks and recreation departments, YMCAs, and individuals develop basketball programs for all skill levels. The YBOA provides information on league development, tournaments, coaching clinics, and scholarship programs. Benefits of membership include insurance, publications, and team discounts.
www.yboa.org

Websites and Electronic Newsletters

Basketball Highway
www.bbhighway.com
The Basketball Highway website offers a public forum, resources for coaches, links to other valuable websites, and opportunities to purchase quality instructional materials for coaches.

Bruce Brown
www.proactivecoaching.info
This website was developed around the philosophy of coaching for both character and competence. It offers books, booklets, videos, presentations, and audio CDs by Bruce Brown for coaches, athletes, administrators, parents, and athletic leaders.

Coaches Choice

www.coacheschoice.com

Coaches Choice is one of the leading producers of informational coaching material for all sports. They offer an extensive selection of books, videos, and DVDs that provide valuable information on offense, defense, practice planning, player development, motivation, and more.

Jerry Krause

www.coachjerrykrause.com

This website offers easy access to all of the books and videos authored by Jerry Krause. Dr. Krause's site also offers some of his personal coaching philosophy and information on coaching ethics.

Guide to Coaching Basketball

www.guidetocoachingbasketball.com

This website offers basketball coaching tools and drills. In addition, it gives a coaching philosophy and provides useful clip art such as a basketball court diagrams.

Power Basketball

www.powerbasketball.com

Power Basketball provides a variety of articles that aim to improve individual and team basketball skills. An assortment of newsletters can be subscribed to through this site.

Sports Parents

www.sportsparents.com

Through this website, browsers are granted access to many articles from *Sports Parents* magazine, with topics ranging from coaching, sportsmanship, and nutrition to equipment, safety, and finance. A parents' tips section helps parents deal with serious sports-related topics such as sibling rivalry, self-esteem, and sports-related eating disorders.

World of Sports: Youth Sports on the World Wide Web

www.worldofsports.com

The World of Sports website acts as a switchboard for many other youth sports websites. It also provides a busy and interesting coaches forum.

D

Games Approach to Teaching Sport Skills

The most common method for teaching sports skills uses the following steps:
- Demonstration/explanation by coaches
- Player imitation of demonstrations
- Coaches' correction of imitations
- Repetition, repetition, repetition

Movement skills are practiced with the goal of "game skills at game speed." Players are encouraged to do the skill correctly first, increase their speed until a rhythm is reached, and continue toward game speed until mistakes are made (providing status and progress reports). Some coaches criticize this method as the "skill-drill-kill desire" approach, but it is effective when combined with positive coaching.

An alternative method that has gained some popularity is termed the "games approach" to learning. Basically, this approach uses the following format:
- Competition/playing first—playing a modified game focused on specific skills (find a need that requires correction)
- The coach stops play when the need is discovered by the coach and players. Fill the need with "skills and drills" work to address the different skill.
- Return to competition/play by practicing the identified skills in modified or full games.

An example of this games approach to coaching involves a focus on the skill of shooting lay-ups on offense. With this focus in every player's mind, modified play begins in a three-on-three half-court game with the goal of only scoring by lay-ups. After a few minutes of play, the coach stops play to point out the difficulty of getting (and hitting) lay-ups. In this way, players discover a need to be able to get and hit lay-ups. The skills and drills method of learning skills is then used to teach lay-up skills. Finally, after skills are practiced and learned, a return to modified games and play takes place—starting with a two-on-one modified game followed by a return to the three-on-three half-court game while trying to score lay-ups.

A number of modified games exist that coaches can develop to teach all offensive and defensive skills. On offense, some suggestions for modified games are:
- Ballhandling emphasis (pass, catch, dribble)
  - ✓ Three-on-three/four-on-four half-court with a designated number of passes
  - ✓ One-on-one/two-on-two/three-on-three half-court with scoring from a dribble drive
  - ✓ Three-on-three pass and cut to the basket
  - ✓ Two-on-one/three-on-two games to emphasize player movement
  - ✓ Three-on-three half-court with a designated number of passes (e.g., 10), with or without a dribble. This technique focuses on offensive spacing and spreading the floor.
- Shooting games
  - ✓ Lay-ups only
  - ✓ Designated number of passes
- Scoring from a rebound
- Special situations
  - ✓ Free throws
  - ✓ Out-of-bounds plays
  - ✓ Rebound situations
  - ✓ Screening

Defensive skills can also be taught and practiced using the games approach. Some examples of modified games for defense are:
- Defending the ball (live, dribble)
  - ✓ One-on-one half-court

✓One-on-one full-court (can also use an extra defender to build confidence: one-on-two)
- Defending off the ball
  ✓Two-on-two/three-on-three half-court (can limit the offense: number of dribbles, no dribble, number of passes)
- Defending the post
- Special situations

Basketball Terminology

Advancing the ball—Before a shot at the basket can be tried, a team must move the ball from one end of the playing court to the other. The ball may be legally advanced by passing or dribbling.

Air ball—An attempted shot at the basket that sails through the air and fails to touch the rim, net, or backboard

Arc—The path of a ball on a shot to the basket. The ball should curve up before it comes down into the basket. Also, the three-point field goal court marking is sometimes called the arc.

Backboard—The rectangular or semicircular fan-shaped surface on which the basket is mounted, used for bank shots. It is also called the glass, if so constructed. In outside lots, it's usually made of wood or metal. The backboard has also been called a bankboard or a bangboard.

Backcourt—The half of the court farthest from your basket. In the early days, some players stayed back on defense all of the time, by rule, and were called backcourt players. Now the term is used to describe the area itself, and the offence can't take the ball into the backcourt area once they completely cross the midcourt line (also called the backcourt line).

Backdoor play—An offensive move in which a closely guarded player runs away from the basket to receive a pass, then suddenly reverses direction and heads for the basket to receive the pass.

Ball—A basketball is perfectly round and may be made of rubber or leather. Its circumference is 29-1/2 to 30 inches. Long ago, basketballs were made of stitched leather. Today's basketballs are molded and have smooth surfaces.

Ballhandling—Passing, catching, dribbling, and controlling the ball without losing possession

Bank shot—A shot, usually taken from an angle, that bounces against the backboard just above the rim and falls into the basket

Baseball pass—A one-handed pass thrown with the same overhand motion used to throw a baseball. It is often used as the first pass of a fast break.

Baseline—The line and the floor area from sideline to sideline under each basket.

Basket—The 18-inch circumference hoop that players shoot at (also known as a bucket). When the ball goes through, it is a field goal and one, two, or three points are awarded.

Blocked shot—An attempted shot at the basket that is knocked away by a defensive player after the ball has left the hand of the shooter and before the ball has started to come down into the basket (also called a rejection)

Blocking—An illegal play or screen that impedes the progress of an opponent

Blocking out—Used by defensive players to keep the offensive players away from the basket after a missed shot. The defensive players turn their backs into the offensive players and block them away from the basket area (also called boxing out).

Bounce pass—A pass that is bounced on the floor from one offensive player to another

Breakaway—When a player runs down-court ahead of the other team and receives a pass from a teammate. This play is used as part of a fast break.

Center—This offensive player, also called the pivot player, plays near the basket. The center is usually the tallest player on a team.

Center jump—An official tosses the ball up between the best jumpers of each team, usually the centers, and each jumper tries to tap the ball to his teammates. The players must tap the ball, not grab it. The other members of both teams must stay outside the center circle during the jump. The center jump is used to begin play at the start of a game.

Charge—A player-control foul committed by a driving offensive player running into a stationary defender who has established his position. The defense gets possession.

Charity stripe—Another name for the free throw line

Chest pass—A two-handed pass thrown from chest level

Clear out—Four offensive players moving to one side of the playing court to allow their remaining teammate to make a play b himself. This gives the remaining offensive player a larger area in which to make a play.

Coach—The organizer, teacher, and leader of a team. The coach sits on the players' bench during a game and plans and directs the team's strategy.

Conditioning—Exercises and drills used by a coach to put his team in top physical condition

Court—Another term for the basketball playing area

Crash the boards—Running to the hoop after a shot to get a rebound

Crossover dribble—This play is used by a player with the ball to change the direction in which he is dribbling and to confuse the defensive players nearest him. The player dribbling the ball suddenly bounces the ball from one hand/side to the other hand/side, and continues to dribble with his other hand.

Cutting—Moving quickly toward the basket hoping to receive a pass from a teammate

Defense—Trying to stop the other team from scoring or advancing the ball and getting ball possession for your team

Double dribble—Dribbling again after having already stopped. Also, dribbling with two hands at the same time. Both types of double dribbling are illegal.

Double-team—Two defensive players guarding one offensive player

Dribbling—Moving the ball across the floor by bouncing it. When a player taps the ball with one hand so that it bounces on the floor, this is called a dribble. A player can dribble once or any number of times before stopping. Once stopped, the player cannot continue dribbling.

Drive—When an offensive player with the ball dribbles to the basket for a lay-up shot

Dunking the ball—An offensive play in which a player with the ball jumps and jams the ball down into the basket

End lines—The lines under each basket that connect the sidelines. The end line is also called the baseline.

Fakes and feints—Tricky moves of the eyes, head, ball, and/or body that are used to throw an opponent off balance

Fast break—A type of offense used to move the ball quickly toward the basket while trying to outnumber the defense before the defensive team can get there to prevent the play. It begins as soon as a team gets the ball.

Field goal—A successful attempt at the basket, but not a free throw. A field goal counts two or three points (when shot behind the arc).

Floating a pass—Making a high, soft pass that is easy to intercept

Follow-through—Following the flight of the ball with the arms after passing or shooting

Footwork—Moving using the feet to carry out a basketball stance, starts, steps, jumps, and stops

Forward—Another term for the corner position on a team

Foul—An infraction or breaking of the rules for which a penalty is charged

Free throw—A free shot given to a player because of a foul by the opposing team. This shot is taken from the free throw line, which is 15 feet from the backboard.

Free-throw lane—The area inside the large rectangle under each basket. On offense, a player cannot remain inside this area for more than three seconds at a time. Players often run across this area looking for passes from their teammates. In amateur basketball the lane is 12 feet wide.

Free-throw line—A line in front of each basket where players stand to shoot free throws. The line is 15 feet from the backboard.

Full court—The entire court area from end line to end line

Fundamentals—The basic rules, strategy, and techniques of basketball

Give-and-go—An offensive play in which one player gives the ball to a teammate and then runs to the basket looking for a return pass.

Guard—A member of the offensive team who plays away from the basket and directs the offensive system. Guards are usually quick on their feed and good ball handlers and/or shooters.

Half-court—One of the two halves of the court on either side of the division line

Halftime—The rest period between the two halves. High school teams rest for 10 minutes. College and professional teams have 15-minute rest periods at halftime.

Held ball—When a player from each team grabs the ball at the same time with one or both hands

Holding—Personal contact with an opponent that interferes with a player's freedom of movement: an illegal act which, when detected, results in a foul

Hoop—Another term for basket

Hustling—Playing with extra effort on both offense and defense

Inside play—Offensive plays and strategies that take place in the area under the basket; also called post play

Jump shot—The most popular shot in basketball. A player stops, jumps, and, at the highest point of his jump, tosses the ball at the hoop.

Key—The free-throw lane and the jump-ball circle attached to it. The shape of this area used to resemble a keyhole.

Lay-up—A shot at the basket from directly under, or from the side of, the basket. This shot can be attempted after dribbling to the basket or after receiving a pass.

Loose ball—When neither team has possession of a bouncing or rolling ball

Man-to-man or player-to-player defense—A defensive system in which each player guards a definite player on the opposing team. The defensive players try to keep their opponents from shooting and passing.

Midcourt line—A line dividing the playing court into halves. Once the offensive team crosses this line with the ball, it cannot take the ball back across the line.

Net—Made of white chord and hung from the rim of each basket, the net slows down the ball as it passes through the hoop.

Offense—The team trying to score or put the ball through the basket

Offensive foul or charge—When a player on the offensive team charges into or blocks a member of the defensive team

Officials—The referee(s) and umpire who are on the court. All use whistles to call attention to their signals. The timer and scorekeeper assist them and occupy positions at the scorer's table.

Open shot—When a player with the ball is in good position to shoot and is not being bothered by defensive players

Out of bounds—Outside of the end lines and sidelines. When a player's foot touches or goes past one of these lines, he is out of bounds.

Outside play—An offensive scoring play that begins away from the basket; also called perimeter play

Overhead pass—A pass thrown from above the head with the arms fully extended

Overtime—An extra period of play needed to decide the winner of a tie game

Personal foul—Another term for foul. Each player is allowed only a certain number of personal fouls before he becomes disqualified. Disqualified players must leave the game.

Pick or screen—A legal block of a defensive player by an offensive player. When the player making the pick does not have the ball, he cannot move into the path of the moving defensive player too quickly. If he has the ball, he can pivot and make a legal block while handing the ball to a teammate.

Pick and roll—An offensive play performed by two members of the offensive team. One player makes a pick then hands the ball to a teammate. After handing off, the player who made the pick heads for the basket hoping to receive a pass. Going to the basket after making a pick is called rolling to the basket.

Pivoting—Making a turn on one foot. This foot, the pivot foot, must always be in contact with the floor. A pivot can be made with or without the ball.

Pivot player—Another term for a center or post. This player is usually tall and he usually plays near the basket.

Press or pressing defense—A system in which the defensive players guard the other team's offensive players very closely to cause them to make bad passes or shots. This system can be played full- or half-court.

Rebounding—Going after and getting the ball after any player has missed a basket. Both the offensive team and the defensive team try to get the missed shot. Much body contact results under the basket as players from both teams crowd each other to retrieve the ball.

Referee—One of the officials on the court who makes sure the game is played according to the rules

Running a play—Executing or performing an offensive play

Safety player—The offensive player who stays near the midcourt line while his teammates are running a play and shooting. This player guards against a quick fast break by the other team.

Scoring—All successful baskets and free throws players make during a game. Each successful basket, also called a field goal, counts for two or three points, and each successful free throw counts for one point.

Sidelines—The long lines on the side of the playing court that connect the end lines. Any play on, or outside of, these lines is out of bounds

Statistics—A written record of shots, rebounds, assists, errors, etc., that is used by coaches and sportswriters to evaluate teams

Substitutes—Extra members of a team who sit on the players' bench with the coach. These players enter the game when their teammates on the floor need a rest or have fouled too many times and are disqualified from the game.

Teamwork—Players of a team working together to score baskets and to stop the other team from scoring

Three-point play—An offensive play in which a player makes a successful try for a basket and is fouled at the same time. The player then sinks a free throw for a total of three points.

Three-point field goal—A successful shot taken past the three point line (arc)

Time-out—A period of time in which the game clock is stopped for reason of injury, assessing fouls, or shooting free throws. A team may also call a time-out to rest its players or to talk about strategy.

Trap—When two defensive players double-team an offensive player who has the ball. They harass the player and try to cause him to make a bad pass or shot.

Traveling—When an offensive player illegally advances the ball by running or walking with it. The referee then blows his whistle, stops play, and gives the ball to the other team.

Turnovers—Errors that cause the offensive team to lose possession of the ball. The ball is then "turned over" to the opponents.

Umpire and referee—The officials who are on the court enforcing playing rules

V-cut or fake and break—An offensive move used to escape a defensive player to receive a pass. The offensive player making this move runs a few steps toward the basket, then suddenly changes direction and heads toward a teammate with the ball. The path the player takes is V-shaped.

Violations—Infractions of the rules that result in loss of the ball rather than in free throws. Traveling, three seconds in the lane, and carrying the ball are common violations.

X's and O's—The symbols used by coaches when drawing plays on a blackboard. The X's usually represent the defensive players and the O's represent the offensive players.

Zone defense—A type of defense in which each defensive player guards a certain area of the court rather than an individual offensive player

About the Authors

Jerry Krause is the director of basketball operations for the Gonzaga University men's basketball team. Krause has taught and coached basketball for more than 40 years and is recognized as a master teacher and clinician. He is the most prolific author in the history of basketball, having written or edited 31 books and developed over 30 instructional videos. He is the chairman of the NABC Research Committee and former chair of the NABC Rules Committee.

In 2000, Krause was inducted to the NAIA Basketball Coaches Hall of Fame and the National Association for Sports and Physical Educators Hall of Fame as a coach and physical educator. Most recently, he was inducted into the Eastern Washington University Hall of Fame as a coach.

Bruce Brown is the director of Proactive Coaching (www.proactivecoaching.info) and special presenter for the NAIA Champions of Character program. He speaks regularly on the subjects of character and teamwork. Brown worked in the state of Washington for more than 35 years as a teacher, coach, and athletic administrator at the junior high, high school, junior college, and college levels.

Bruce has written seven books and 10 coaching booklets and has produced 12 instructional videos. In 2002, he received NAIA Co-National Athletic Director of the Year honors, and in 2003 was given the Citizenship Through Sports Alliance National Award for Lifetime Achievement. Brown also received the Coach Krzyzewski Leadership Award from the College of the Ozarks in 2004.

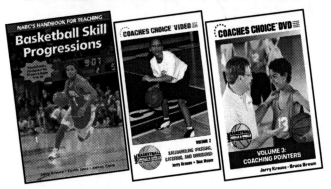